Books are to be returned on or before
the last date below.

CONSTRUCTION
ADJUDICATION

CONSTRUCTION ADJUDICATION

Richard Mills

Acknowledgement

Crown copyright material is reproduced with the permission of the Controller of HMSO and the Queen's Printer for Scotland.

Please note: References to the masculine include, where appropriate, the feminine.

Published by RICS Business Services Limited
a wholly owned subsidiary of
The Royal Institution of Chartered Surveyors
under the RICS Books imprint
Surveyor Court
Westwood Business Park
Coventry CV4 8JE
UK
www.ricsbooks.com

ISBN 1 84219 235 3

Typeset in Great Britain by Columns Design Ltd, Reading
Printed in Great Britain by Bell & Bain, Glasgow

Contents

Contents

Preface

While chartered surveyors do not normally need the *breadth* of understanding of the law of their opposite numbers in the legal profession, in a number of key areas of application to construction and property they need a similar *depth* of legal knowledge. Exactly what the key areas may be depends to some extent on the nature of the surveyor's practice. An obvious example is the law relating to party walls. There are certainly specialist surveyors who, apart from the procedural aspects of the *Party Wall etc. Act* 1996, would actually know more about the case law on the Act than the average lawyer in general practice.

So surveyors need law and, for a variety of reasons, need to maintain and develop their understanding of it. Changing trends or individual variations in clients' requirements mean that from time to time even the best practitioners (perhaps especially the best practitioners) will feel the need to expand their knowledge. The knowledge acquired at college or in studying for the Assessment of Professional Competence ('APC') has a limited shelf life and needs to be constantly updated to maintain its currency. Even specialists working in their areas of expertise need a source of reference as an aide-mémoire or as a first port of call in more detailed research.

The Case in Point Series

RICS Books is committed to meeting the needs of surveying and other professionals and the Case in Point series typifies that commitment. It is aimed at those who need to upgrade their legal knowledge, or update it, or have access to a good first reference point at the outset of an inquiry. A particular difficulty is the burgeoning of reported decisions of the courts. The sheer scale of the law reports, both general and specialist, makes it very hard even to be aware of recent trends, let alone identify the significance of a particular decision. Thus it was decided to focus on developments in case law. In any given matter, the practitioner will want to be directed efficiently and painlessly to the decision that bears upon the matter he or she is dealing with, in other words to – the Case in Point.

The books in the Case in Point series offer a wealth of legal information which is essential in its practical application to the surveyor's work. Authors have been chosen as having the ability to be selective and succinct, thus achieving a high degree of relevance without sacrificing accessibility. The series has developed as a collection of specialist handbooks which can deliver what practitioners need – the law on the matter they are handling, when they want it.

Adjudication, Richard Mills

The *Housing Grants, Construction and Regeneration Act* 1996 is one of the most important pieces of legislation the construction industry has ever been obliged to understand. In addition to its payment provisions, significant enough in themselves, it introduced a new statutory dispute resolution system to the UK's construction industry, namely adjudication. This is not to say that adjudication was unknown before, but the revolutionary step taken was to introduce a mandatory regime which, subject to some categories of exceptions, would apply to all construction contracts. It is of some interest to note that the Australian States, New Zealand and most recently Singapore have also adopted versions of this legislation, by no means identical, but also importing adjudication.

Ironically, but inevitably, adjudication, designed to provide summary justice, has led to prolific litigation in the Technology and Construction Court and, in a few cases, in the Court of Appeal. The construction industry and its professional advisers have had to come to terms with the outcomes in the form of a growing body of case law on almost every aspect, on the adjudication agreement itself, on the reference, on the adjudicator's powers, on procedure, on the decision, on enforcement and on the prospects for legal challenge (which can incorporate any of the above).

It was apparent to RICS Books that the task of digesting and analysing the case law on adjudication would require both legal skills and a strong awareness of the impact of decisions upon construction industry professionals and their clients.

Richard Mills is qualified both as a quantity surveyor (FRICS) and as a solicitor. A former partner of EC Harris and current Chairman of the RICS Ethics Conduct and Consumer Policy Committee, Richard has strong credentials as a construction practitioner. As principal of Mills & Co Solicitors, with an exclusively construction law practice, he is well qualified to consider legal as well as practical implications of case law.

With this background, it is unsurprising that Richard is heavily involved in adjudication, advising contractors, subcontractors, owners and consultants on all aspects of the process. The combination of law and construction which his profile represents mirrors that of adjudication and fits him well for the task of explaining the key cases.

Anthony Lavers, 2005.
White & Case, London.
Visiting Professor of Law, Oxford Brookes University, Oxford.
Consultant Editor, Case in Point Series.

Introduction

Adjudication, as it is defined for the purposes of this casebook, was introduced to the UK construction industry by way of Part II of the *Housing Grants, Construction and Regeneration Act* 1996 – hereafter referred to as 'the Act'. The Act applies to all construction contracts (with some exceptions) made after 1 May 1998.

Two main things happened in response to the provisions of that Act:

Firstly, Statutory Instruments were produced. These set out detailed procedures for adjudication in the event that the parties failed to agree adjudication procedures in their construction contract that were compliant with the requirements of the Act. The relevant Statutory Instruments are collectively referred to as the Scheme for Construction Contracts – hereafter referred to as 'the Scheme'.

Secondly, the publishers of standard forms of construction contracts amended their standard contracts to include adjudication procedures that were compliant with the provisions of the Act. These contracts are sometimes used on construction projects that are outside the scope of the Act.

A considerable body of case law has developed as a result of the introduction of this legislation, the most important of which are captured in this case book. This book is current to the end of July 2005.

In this book the cases have been arranged into a number of subject areas. However, the nature of adjudication is that those seeking to avoid the mandatory effect of an adjudicator's decision will usually raise a number of points on which, they argue, the decision should be set aside. Therefore each decision of the court usually addresses a number of separate points, each of which may fall into a separate subject area. This book deals with this challenge by summarising each case in the chapter in which it is considered to be most appropriate. Cross-references have then been introduced into those other chapters to which the case may also be relevant.

List of Acts, Statutory Instruments/Rules and abbreviations

The following Acts, Statutory Instruments and Statutory Rules are referenced in this publication. Where a piece of legislation is mentioned frequently, it is referred to by the abbreviation that follows the name of the legislation in brackets.

Arbitration Act 1996
Education Act 1996
Employment Rights Act 1996
Exchequer and Audit Departments Act 1866
Highways Act 1980
Housing Grants, Construction and Regeneration Act 1996 (**'the Act'**)
Human Rights Act 1998
Late Payment of Commercial Debts (Interest) Act 1998
Local Government Act (Northern Ireland) Act 1972
Local Government Act etc. (Scotland) Act 1994
National Audit Act 1983
National Health Service (Private Finance) Act 1997
Northern Ireland Act 1974
Party Wall etc. Act 1996
Roads (Scotland) Act 1984
Self-Governing Schools etc. (Scotland) Act 1989
Sewerage (Scotland) Act 1968
Town and Country Planning (Scotland) Act 1997
Town and Country Planning Act 1990
Unfair Contract Terms Act 1977
Water Industry Act 1991

Civil Procedure Rules 1998 (SI 1998/3132)
Construction Contracts (Northern Ireland) Order 1997
Education and Libraries (Northern Ireland) Order 1986
Exclusion Orders:
    Construction Contracts (England and Wales) Exclusion Order 1998
      (SI 1998/648)

Construction Contracts (Scotland) Exclusion Order 1998 (SI 1998/686)

Construction Contracts Exclusion Order (Northern Ireland) 1999 (Statutory Rule 1999/33)

Health and Personal Social Services (Northern Ireland) Order 1972

Health and Personal Social Services (Private Finance) (Northern Ireland) Order 1977

Planning (Northern Ireland) Order 1991

Private Streets (Northern Ireland) Order 1980

Roads (Northern Ireland) Order 1993

Rules of the Supreme Court 1965

The Scheme for Construction Contracts (**'the Scheme'**):

Scheme for Construction Contracts (England and Wales) Regulations 1998 (SI 1998/649)

Scheme for Construction Contracts (Scotland) Regulations 1998 (SI 1998/687)

Scheme for Construction Contracts in Northern Ireland Regulations (Northern Ireland) 1999 (Statutory Rule 1999/32)

Unfair Terms in Consumer Contracts Regulations 1999 (SI 1999/2083)

Water and Sewerage Services (Northern Ireland) Order 1973

The text of this publication is divided into commentary and case summaries. The commentary is enclosed between grey highlighted lines for ease of reference.

Table of cases

A number of case reports are available on the internet. In such cases the marks * and † denote the following:

* report available at www.bailii.org
† report available at www.adjudication.co.uk

1
Statutory adjudication

The *Housing Grants, Construction and Regeneration Act* 1996 ('the Act') applies to contracts for the carrying out of construction operations in England, Wales, Northern Ireland or Scotland. The Act also applies to agreements to provide architectural, design or surveying work or to provide advice on building, engineering, interior or exterior decoration or on the laying out of landscape, in relation to construction operations.

The Act does not apply to:

- contracts with residential occupiers;
- contracts that are not in writing;
- assembly, installation or demolition of plant and machinery or its supporting steelwork on a site where the primary activity is nuclear processing, power generation, water or effluent treatment, or the processing or storing of chemicals, pharmaceuticals, oil, gas, steel, food or drink;
- the supply only of building or engineering components or equipment or materials or plant or machinery except under a contract that also provides for their installation;
- the drilling for or extraction of oil or natural gas or minerals;
- the making, installation or repair of artistic works.

The Act also does not apply to:

- contracts entered into under the private finance initiative;
- finance agreements;
- development agreements.

These latter items are further defined by the Exclusion Orders, copies of which are included at the end of this book.

1.1 THE MAKING OF A CONSTRUCTION CONTRACT

Only disputes arising under construction contracts made after 1 May 1998 can be adjudicated.

Shepherd Construction Ltd v Mecright Ltd (2000)

The parties were parties to a construction contract under which a dispute had arisen. The parties had settled their dispute pursuant to a settlement agreement. However, Mecright sought subsequently to adjudicate on the dispute, arguing that it had only entered into the settlement agreement under duress.

Shepherd Construction sought a declaration from the court that the settlement agreement meant that there was no dispute arising under the subcontract capable of being referred to adjudication; and further, that that duress claim was not a dispute capable of adjudication.

The court decided in favour of Shepherd, giving both declarations sought. The court decided that a dispute as to the terms of the settlement agreement was not a dispute arising under a construction contract.

Workplace Technologies plc v E Squared Ltd and Mr J L Riches (2000)

This case concerned the principal question of whether or not the construction contract was made before or after the Act came into force – 1 May 1998. E Squared sought to refer the dispute that had arisen under the contract to adjudication.

Workplace Technologies sought a declaration to the effect that the contract came into force before 1 May 1998; a declaration as to the terms of the contract, a declaration that the adjudicator had no jurisdiction; and an injunction to prevent the referring party from continuing with the adjudication.

The judge concluded on the facts of this case that he could not give the declarations sought. This case involved a continuum of negotiations with each party making various proposals and counter-proposals from late 1997 to June 1998. The judge concluded that following the proposal to use the Gold Form on 20 May 1998 it was significant that there is no suggestion that any other amendment to the form, other than the filling in of the blanks, seems to have been contemplated.

This was evidenced by a letter dated 5 June 1998, which accepted that obligation without qualification or rider. The judge was therefore satisfied that it was not until, at the earliest, 20 May, but certainly by 5 June that the contract between the parties was ultimately concluded.

The judge also concluded that he was not persuaded that there is power to grant an injunction to restrain a party initiating a void reference and pursuing proceedings that themselves are void and that may give rise to a void, and thus an unenforceable, adjudication decision. There does not appear to be any legal or equitable interest such as an injunction would protect. Doubtless the initiation of such proceedings may be conceived to be a source of harassment, pressure or needless expense.

Earls Terrace Properties Ltd v Waterloo Investments Ltd (2002)

A contract was concluded between the parties in 1996 which it was accepted for the purposes of this case amounted to a construction contract; but, as the contract was made before the Act came into force, the Act was not applicable. However, in 1998, after the Act came into force, the parties entered into a deed varying the terms of the original contract. Disputes arose, which the defendant sought to refer to adjudication. This action was brought under Part 8 of the *Civil Procedure Rules* 1998 (SI 1998/3132) to determine as a point of law whether or not the Act applied to the contract.

The court found that the deed by itself was not a construction contract, as the services that were to be provided were not altered by the deed. The variations that were made in the deed were simply to sums of money that were payable.

His Honour Judge Seymour therefore concluded that:

'The question, then, is whether the effect of the making of the Agreement of the 20th of July 1998, not itself being a construction contract, but which varied the terms of the agreement dated the 4th of December 1996, which was a construction contract, but not a

3

construction contract to which the provisions of the Act applied, was to bring within Part II of the Housing Grants, Construction and Regeneration Act 1996 the Agreement dated the 4th of December 1996. In my judgement, that would be a rather bizarre consequence.'

However, see also *Christiani & Nielsen Ltd v The Lowry Centre Development Company Ltd* (2000), summarised at 1.9, in which the court concluded that the deed superseded the earlier letter of intent and was not merely an agreement to vary the contract made in a letter of intent. Therefore the contract set out in the deed was made after 1 May 1998.

1.2 CONTRACTUAL INTERPRETATION

Interpretation of the construction contract is a matter that is within the adjudicator's jurisdiction.

Tim Butler Contractors Ltd v Merewood Homes Ltd (2000)

The responding party challenged the decision of the adjudicator on the basis that he had decided in favour of the referring party and had awarded payment by instalments. The responding party asserted that the construction contract was for a period of fewer than 45 days and therefore the referring party had no right to payment by instalments. The court decided that the question of whether a construction contract came into existence that entitled the claimant to staged payments was a dispute as to the terms of the contract, and not a dispute that went to jurisdiction of the adjudicator. Therefore the court could not open up and review the adjudicator's decision on this point.

See also *Watson Building Services Ltd* (2001), summarised at 2.4, in which the judge considered that the adjudicator had the power to determine the meaning and import of the subcontract terms, even where such an exercise resulted in his determining a dispute about the validity of his appointment and, in effect, his jurisdiction.

1.3 CONTRACTS IN WRITING

The requirement for construction contracts to be in writing before the Act applies has been interpreted as requiring all of the relevant terms to be in writing.

Maymac Environmental Services Ltd v Faraday Building Services Ltd (2000)

Having been through an adjudication and having lost, Faraday sought to defend enforcement proceedings on the basis that there was no contract in writing for the purposes of the Act. The court concluded that in fact there was overwhelming evidence that the parties had reached agreement on the terms on which they agreed to be bound and, as the contract progressed and further details were agreed, they also agreed to be bound by those further terms. There was thus a concluded contract.

Further, the court found that Faraday had in any event explicitly argued before the adjudicator that his jurisdiction was limited to Maymac's entitlement to payment under their application for payment number two. They therefore accepted the adjudicator's jurisdiction to determine the dispute that Maymac had referred to the adjudicator and on which the adjudicator made his decision.

Debeck Ductworth Installations Ltd v T&E Engineering Ltd (2002)

In this case the parties concluded an oral contract that the claimant asserted was evidenced in writing by way of a fax which they claimed contained all relevant terms of the agreement. These submissions were rejected by the court on two counts, following and interpreting the decision of the Court of Appeal in *RJT Consulting Engineers Ltd v DM Engineering Northern Ireland Ltd* (2002): Firstly, the court found that the fax did not in fact set out or record all of those matters on which the claimant itself was seeking to rely in pursuing its claim. The fax did not explain, even in summary terms, the scope of the work to be undertaken. Secondly, the court was satisfied by evidence given by the defendant that there were further terms of the contract agreed between the parties and on which the defendant relied.

RJT Consulting Engineers Ltd v DM Engineering (Northern Ireland) Ltd (2002), CA

The appellant, RJT Consulting Engineers Ltd, was a practice of consulting engineers. It was retained by the Holiday Inn, Liverpool, to provide the outline design for mechanical and electrical work that was to be undertaken as part of the refurbishment of the hotel. The main contractor engaged the respondent, DM Engineering (NI) Ltd, as the mechanical and electrical subcontractor. The consultant engineers became involved with the subcontractors in the negotiation to establish a price for that work, eventually agreed at about £1.8m. The subcontracted works included completion of some design, and DM Engineering asked RJT if the consultants would complete the design on their behalf. A fee of £12,000 was agreed.

DM Engineering subsequently claimed some £858,000 from RJT for alleged negligent design and/or breach of contract and sought to refer the dispute to adjudication. The appellants challenged the right to seek adjudication, denying that the agreement was in writing and within Part II of the Act.

At first instance the judge found that there was sufficient evidence in writing of a contract for the purposes of section 107 of the Act. This judgment was appealed.

In the Court of Appeal Lord Justice Ward found as follows:

> 'On the point of construction of section 107, what has to be evidenced in writing is, literally, the agreement, which means all of it, not part of it. A record of the agreement also suggests a complete agreement, not a partial one. The only exception to the generality of that construction is the instance falling within sub-section 5 where the material or relevant parts alleged and not denied in the written submissions in the adjudication proceedings are sufficient. Unfortunately, I do not think sub-section 5 can so dominate the interpretation of the

section as a whole so as to limit what needs to be evidenced in writing simply to the material terms raised in the arbitration. It must be remembered that by virtue of section 107(1) the need for an agreement in writing is the precondition for the application of the other provisions of Part II of the Act, not just the jurisdictional threshold for a reference to adjudication. I say "unfortunately" because, like Auld L.J. whose judgment I have now read in draft, I would regard it as a pity if too much "jurisdictional wrangling" were to limit the opportunities for expeditious adjudication having an interim effect only. No doubt adjudicators will be robust in excluding the trivial from the ambit of the agreement and the matter must be entrusted to their common sense. Here we have a comparatively simple oral agreement about the terms of which there may be very little, if any, dispute. For the consulting engineers to take a point objecting to adjudication in those circumstances may be open to the criticism that they were taking a technical point but as it was one open to them and it is good, they cannot be faulted. In my judgment they were entitled to the declaration which they sought and I would accordingly allow the appeal and grant them that relief.'

Lord Justice Auld agreed that the appeal should be allowed, but not because the whole agreement was not in writing in any of the forms for which section 107 of the 1996 Act makes provision, but because the material terms of the agreement were insufficiently recorded in writing in any of those forms.

Pegram Shopfitters Ltd v Tally Wiejl (UK) Ltd (2003), CA

Both parties contended that there was a construction contract in being, but were at odds as to the terms and conditions that applied to it – each having promoted their own terms at different times. But it was the defendant's crystal clear contention, both before the adjudicator and before the judge, that, if no contract was concluded on the JCT Prime Cost Terms, there was no contract at all and the claimants were entitled to be paid a reasonable sum for the work they had carried out.

7

Both the adjudicator and the first instance judge proceeded along the lines that both parties were contending that a construction contract existed (even though they were proposing that different contracts applied) and that the Act therefore applied to their contract. However, such a conclusion ignored the defendant's alternative contention that if the terms that they proposed did not apply, then there was no contract in place.

The Court of Appeal found in favour of the defendant's argument that summary judgment should not be given in favour of the claimant because the defendant had a real, not fanciful, prospect of establishing that the adjudicator acted without jurisdiction. It was argued that the adjudicator was appointed under the provisions of the Scheme for Construction Contracts when the Scheme did not apply; because on one view there was no written construction contract within section 107 of the 1996 Act at all; and because he had no jurisdiction to determine his own jurisdiction.

Branlow Ltd v Dem-Master Demolition Ltd (2004)

Having concluded that all of the material terms of the contract were contained in two letters, the court found that this was sufficient to bring the contract within the provisions of the Act. The defenders had argued that the Act required certainty in the agreed terms, which the two letters did not provide. The court did not agree with this interpretation.

GPN Ltd (In Receivership) v O2 (UK) Ltd (2004)

The claimant made an application to enforce the decision of an adjudicator by way of summary judgment. The defendant successfully argued that the claim should be struck out as showing no real prospect of success because there was no contract in writing between the parties. The contract upon which the claimant sought to rely had been negotiated between themselves and the quantity surveyors appointed on behalf of the defendant, but had never been signed by the parties. The court found that the quantity surveyors had neither actual nor ostensible authority to bind their client. Therefore there was no contract in writing.

Trustees of the Stratfield Saye Estate v AHL Construction Ltd (2004)

In this case a dispute arose on a third adjudication in respect of the same project as to whether or not there was a contract in writing. His Honour Judge Rupert Jackson, having considered the decision of the Court of Appeal in *RJT Consulting Engineers v DM Engineering (Northern Ireland) Ltd* (2002), concluded:

> 'The principle of law which I derive from the majority judgments in *RJT* is this: an agreement is only evidenced in writing for the purposes of section 107, subsections (2), (3) and (4), if all the express terms of that agreement are recorded in writing. It is not sufficient to show that all terms material to the issues under adjudication have been recorded in writing.'

Applying this principle, he found that there was sufficient written evidence of the contract in this case. He then went on to conclude that even if he were wrong, the arguments between the parties in two previous adjudications was sufficient evidence of a contract in writing.

1.4 CONTRACTS FOR THE SUPPLY OF FURNITURE AND SHOP FITTINGS

The Act does not apply to contracts for the provision of furniture that does not become a fixture.

Gibson Lea Retail Interiors Ltd v Makro Self-Service Wholesalers Ltd (2001)

The claimants supplied and installed shop fittings to the defendants' cash-and-carry wholesale business. All of the fittings were designed to be moveable and many were free-standing.

Disputes arose as to payment, which the claimants sought to refer to adjudication. The defendants challenged their rights to do so on the basis that the contract was not one for construction operations within the scope of the Act. The claimants therefore sought a declaration that they were entitled to refer the dispute to adjudication.

When considering whether a contract for the supply and installation of such fittings was within the scope of the Act, the court drew upon established law as to what amounts to 'fixtures and fittings' for assistance. The judge found that in the context of the law of real property, the concept of a fixture is well-established, and applied that concept to the definition of 'construction operations' in section 105(1) of the Act. In the law of real property, one of the factors that is relevant to a determination of whether a chattel attached to a building is a fixture or not is whether the attachment is intended to be permanent.

Applying this test to the facts of the case, the judge concluded that the supply and installation of moveable and free-standing shop fittings were not 'construction operations' within the scope of the Act and therefore declined to give the declaration sought by the claimants.

1.5 MAINTENANCE AND REPAIR OF M&E INSTALLATIONS

However, the Act does apply to the maintenance of gas appliances in residential properties.

Nottingham Community Housing Association Ltd v Powerminster Ltd (2000)

The parties contracted for Powerminster to service and maintain the gas appliances in Nottingham's properties. Disputes arose as to payment, which Powerminster sought to refer to adjudication under the Act. Nottingham argued that the contract was not a contract for construction operations and sought a declaration to this effect. The principal argument related to the interpretation of section 105(1)(a) and (c) of the Act, which provides:

> '105. – (1) In this Part "construction operations" means, subject as follows, operations of any of the following descriptions–

(a) construction, alteration, repair, maintenance, extension, demolition or dismantling of buildings, or structures forming, or to form, part of the land (whether permanent or not); ...

(c) installation in any building or structure of fittings forming part of the land, including (without prejudice to the foregoing) systems of heating, lighting, air-conditioning, ventilation, power supply, drainage, sanitation, water supply or fire protection, or security or communications systems ...'

Nottingham sought to draw a distinction between paragraphs (a) and (c), arguing that the limitation in paragraph (c) to installation displayed an intention on the part of the drafters to exclude repair and maintenance of the listed systems from the terms of paragraph (a).

The court disagreed with Nottingham, finding that the repair and maintenance of gas appliances was clearly within the scope of paragraph (a) and declined to depart from what it considered to be a clear and true meaning because of the presence of paragraph (c).

1.6 PROCESS PLANTS

The Act excludes from the definition of 'construction operations' the:

'... assembly, installation or demolition of plant or machinery, or erection or demolition of steelwork for the purposes of supporting or providing access to plant or machinery, on a site where the primary activity is–

(i) nuclear processing, power generation, or water or effluent treatment, or

(ii) the production, transmission, processing or bulk storage (other than warehousing) of chemicals, pharmaceuticals, oil, gas, steel or food and drink' (section 105(2)(c)).

This is referred to generally as the 'process plant exception'. There have been many cases on the question of whether works come within the process plant exception.

Homer Burgess Ltd v Chirex (Annan) Ltd (1999)

The work of Homer Burgess involved the installation of pipework linking various pieces of equipment. It was common ground between the parties that the site fell within the exception in section 105(2)(c) of the Act, so the only issue remaining was whether the pipework was 'plant' or not.

In considering his own jurisdiction, the adjudicator had recourse to his personal expertise in the process and engineering industry and concluded that in that industry pipework was not ordinarily regarded as plant.

The court took consideration of the fact that 'plant' was not defined within the Act but that it was a phrase that has been used in legislation for well over 100 years. In particular, the court was referred to a long line of cases that concluded that 'plant' was anything by means of which the operations of the business will perform, as distinct from the setting for premises in which the operations took place. This was the test adopted by the court in *CIR v Barclay Curle* (2004) which led to the conclusion that a dry dock was part of the plant rather than part of the premises. The court therefore concluded that the adjudicator was wrong to rely on a special meaning of the word within the process and engineering industry (assuming that the conclusion of applying his own personal expertise was shared by fellow practitioners within that industry), but instead should have applied the general meaning of the word defined by the 'tax' cases predating the Act.

The court concluded that the pipework was clearly part of the plant being assembled or installed on the site. Without such pipework, the individual pieces of machinery or equipment would be unable to operate. The pipework is in a real sense part of the apparatus which, once it was installed, was going to be used in order to carry out the business of manufacturing pharmaceuticals. Therefore, the installation of pipework was an operation that fell within the scope of the exception in section 105(2)(c) of the Act and was accordingly not a construction operation.

Palmers Ltd v ABB Power Construction Ltd (1999)

Palmers were a scaffolding subcontractor to ABB who in turn were appointed to provide heat recovery steam generating boilers and associated pipework at the Esso Fawley Cogeneration Project at Fawley.

Disputes arose between Palmers and ABB, which Palmers sought to refer to adjudication. Concurrently with the referral to adjudication, Palmers issued a notice of intention to suspend performance of their works allegedly pursuant to the provisions of the Act.

ABB retorted that Palmers' contract did not come within the scope of the Act and therefore Palmers had no statutory right to adjudication. Palmers sought to resolve this issue and referred the matter to court for determination on the point of law.

It was accepted by both parties that ABB's own works were outside the scope of the Act pursuant to the exceptions in section 105(2)(c). ABB therefore argued that Palmers' works were also outside the scope of the Act as being operations preparatory to excluded works. The judge disagreed with this interpretation and found that the reference to scaffolding in section 105(1)(e) of the Act referred to the operations in section 105(1) of the Act irrespective of whether the exclusions in section 105(2) applied.

ABB Power Construction Ltd v Norwest Holst Engineering Ltd (2000)

ABB were building three heat recovery steam generators as part of a project to extend an existing power station at Peterhead in Aberdeen. The location where the work was being carried out was separated from the existing power station by 'the Construction Site Fence' and was known for the purposes of the contract as 'the Construction Site', as opposed to 'the Power Station Site'.

Norwest Holst were a subcontractor to ABB for the installation of insulation to clad pipework, drums and various parts of the equipment. The insulation material was provided by ABB.

In considering the interpretation of section 105(2) of the Act, the judge concluded that section 105(2), when compared with section 105(1), showed that it was the intention of parliament that the exemption should be given by applying an additional and different test: was the object of the 'construction operation' to further the activities described in section 105(2)(c) (and in paragraphs (a) and (b)), since in those industries or commercial activities it was not thought necessary that at any level there need to be a right to adjudicate or to payment as provided by the Act.

The judge also said that in his judgment it was clear from the language used in section 105(2) that it was intended that, if the regimes were not to apply, it would be invidious if they applied to some but not all construction contracts on a site or for a project.

The judge concluded that the erection of a fence for operational reasons was irrelevant. He concluded that the fence denotes no more than the customary separation of the 'live' side. He concluded that for the purposes of section 105(2)(c) there is here only one site.

In considering whether the installation of insulation came within the definition of 'plant' for the purposes of the Act, the judge had regard to and adopted the decision in *Homer Burgess Ltd v Chirex (Annan) Ltd* (1999). The judge went on to say that in his judgment any work that would be a 'construction operation' within section 105(1) of the Act and that is necessary for the full and proper assembly or erection of plant so that it will fulfil the purpose or purposes for which it is intended, is exempt by reason of section 105(2)(c) of the Act (assuming that the conditions relating to the site are also satisfied).

One further point raised by ABB but dismissed by the judge was that section 105(2) refers to sites where the primary activity *is* ... etc. ABB therefore asserted that the exceptions in section 105(2)(c) could only apply to sites that were then actually operating according to the primary activity and not to sites that were being constructed with the *intention* or objective of being operated according to the primary activity.

The judge concluded that such an interpretation would lead to an absurdity and that cannot have been the intention of parliament.

ABB Zantingh Ltd v Zedal Building Services Ltd (2000)

In this case the Mirror Group contracted with Scottish Southern Energy (SSE) for the installation of seven large diesel generators on two sites, the principal purpose of which was printing. The combined power of the generators was enough to satisfy the daytime needs of Cheltenham. SSE subcontracted the works to ABB, who in turn subcontracted the supply, installation, labelling, termination and testing of all field wiring including containment and support to Zedal.

These works were undertaken primarily to guarantee the availability of power to the printing works over the 2000 New Year when many companies feared business interruption caused by the 'millennium bug'. The works were not connected to or consequential upon any other works being undertaken at that time at the printing works.

Disputes arose between Zedal and ABB, which Zedal referred to adjudication. ABB sought a declaration from the court that there was no right to adjudicate on the basis that Zedal's works amounted to plant on a site where the primary activity is power generation (the section 105(2)(c) exception).

Following the decisions in *Homer Burgess v Chirex* (1999) and *ABB Power v Norwest Holst* (2000) the judge concluded that Zedal's works did come within the definition of 'plant' for the purposes of the Act.

The question facing the court then was: what was the site? Was it the whole of the printing works, or was it limited to the enclosure within that larger site in which the generating equipment was erected?

The judge concluded that to make sense of the Act one has to look at the nature of the whole site and ask what is the primary purpose of the whole site. Is the primary purpose power generation, or, in this case, printing?

Applying this reasoning, the judge found that the primary purpose of the site was printing, and therefore the work of Zedal did not fall within any exception provided by section 105(2)(c) of the Act.

Mitsui Babcock Energy Services Ltd (2000)

This was a decision of the Court of Session in Scotland, which is therefore strongly persuasive but not binding on the English courts.

The case involved an adjudicator who was appointed by the Royal Institution of Chartered Surveyors (RICS) following an application by Mitsui. On considering the referral she resigned as the adjudicator on the basis that she had no jurisdiction – her lack of jurisdiction arising out of section 105(2)(c) of the Act, which provides that the Act does not apply to assembly, installation or demolition of plant or machinery on a site where the primary activity is the production, transmission, processing or bulk storage of chemicals, pharmaceuticals, oil, gas, steel or food and drink.

Mitsui were installing boilers for the production of steam by a company known as Grangemouth CHP Ltd. The boilers were being installed on land leased from BP that was part of a large petrochemical complex. There were two principal sites for the installation of the boilers, which were separately fenced from the other parts of the complex. One of the sites had its own access, independent of the petrochemical complex.

The issue for determination by the court was what was the definition of the site. If the site was defined by the fenced off areas leased by Grangemouth CHP Ltd, then it did not come within section 105(2)(c) of the Act and the adjudicator was wrong to have resigned. If, however, the site was defined by the petrochemical complex as a whole, then it did come within section 105(2)(c) of the Act and the adjudicator was correct to have resigned.

The court held that the whole petrochemical complex should be considered as forming the site and therefore the adjudicator was correct to have resigned.

In coming to this conclusion, the court considered and adopted the approach taken by Judge Lloyd in *ABB Power Construction Ltd the Norwest Holst Engineering Ltd* (2000), namely:

'... exemption should be given by applying an additional and different test: was the object of the "construction operation" to further the activities described in section 105(2)(c) ... since in those industries or commercial activities it was not thought necessary that at any level there need be a right to adjudicate or to payment as provided by the Act'.

Comsite Projects Ltd v Andritz AG (2003)

Andritz has been appointed on a contract for the installation of a dryer plant and all building services to the dryer building for a new waste water treatment works and sewage sludge recycling centre on the Isle of Wight. Andritz sublet the building services works, comprising mainly lighting, small power, fire alarm and ventilation systems, to Comsite. Austrian law applied to the subcontract and the Austrian courts had exclusive jurisdiction.

This case was brought as a Part 8 claim for a declaration that Comsite's works fell within the definition of construction contracts as set out in section 105 of the Act.

Having established that the English courts had jurisdiction to hear the Part 8 claim, notwithstanding the jurisdiction clause in the contract, the judge went on to consider whether the work undertaken by Comsite amounted to 'construction operations' pursuant to the provisions of the Act. He concluded that as a matter of fact, the building and the services within the building were needed for health and safety reasons and that without them the dryer plant could not lawfully be operated. However, he concluded on the evidence before him that the building and the building services were not needed to enable the plant physically to function. He then concluded that while the installation of electrics, which were an integral part of the dryer plant, would fall within section 105 of the Act, in his judgment the services to the building that were not to be connected into the plant, were not plant of their own right. The fact that the plant may not lawfully operate without some of the services did not mean that the services are integral to the plant and so to fall within the definition of plant in section 105. The judge therefore concluded that the building services subcontract constituted a construction contract as defined in section 104 of the Act, and that therefore both parties had the right to refer the dispute arising under the subcontract to adjudication.

Conor Engineering Ltd v Les Constructions Industrielles de la Mèditerranèe (CNIM) (2004)

CNIM were appointed to construct a waste incineration and power generation plant. Conor were appointed as their subcontractors for the installation of boilers and pipework. Disputes arose between the parties, which Conor referred to adjudication. CNIM refused to pay according to the adjudicator's decision and Conor therefore sought to enforce the decision of the adjudicator pursuant to Part 8 of the *Civil Procedure Rules* 1998.

One of the arguments raised by CNIM was that there was no right to adjudicate as the Scheme was excluded from the provisions of the Act by reason of section 105(2) – the primary activity on the site being power generation. On examination of the facts the court rejected this argument, concluding that power generation was a secondary activity, the primary activity being waste incineration. The court reached this conclusion notwithstanding that the claimant's works were primarily related to the power generation element of the works as a whole.

1.7 CONTRACTS FOR THE SUPPLY ONLY OF MATERIALS, PLANT AND MACHINERY

Contracts for the supply only of materials, plant and machinery are excluded from the scope of the Act (section 105(2)(d)(ii)), but where the contract also includes for the provision of labour those contracts will come within the scope of the provisions of the Act.

In *Baldwins Industrial Service plc v Barr Ltd* (2002), summarised at 11.3, the court concluded that the hire of a 50-tonne crane, together with the driver, to be used by Barr at a building site was not one of mere delivery of plant to site but was for the supply of plant and labour. The contract was therefore a 'construction contract' within the meaning of the Act, and accordingly the adjudicator had jurisdiction.

1.8 CONTRACTS FOR THE PROVISION OF CONSULTANCY SERVICES

The Act has been found to apply to agreements to provide surveying services in relation to construction operations, including allegations of negligence pursuant to those agreements, but not to agreements to provide surveying services in relation to disputes arising under construction contracts.

Fence Gate Ltd v James R Knowles Ltd (2001)

James R. Knowles were appointed to survey a kitchen floor and subsequently to give advice in an arbitration. A dispute arose in connection with their fee, which they sought to refer to adjudication. The court concluded that the survey work was work in connection with construction operations (although no dispute existed in relation to the invoices for this part of the works) but that evidence and advice given in connection with an arbitration was not.

The giving of factual evidence by an architect, designer or surveyor at an arbitration is not the doing of architectural designing or surveyor work itself, and therefore falls outside the scope of the Act.

Where a contract relates both to construction operations and to other activities, the contract is to be treated as severable between those parts that relate to construction operations and those parts that relate to other activities. The Act and the other provisions for adjudication are to apply to the contract only insofar as the contract relates to construction operations.

Gillies Ramsay Diamond and others v PJW Enterprises Ltd (2003)

In this case the court upheld an adjudicator's decision that a contract administrator had been negligent and should pay damages, even though the court doubted the correctness of the adjudicator's finding of negligence.

See also *London & Amsterdam Properties Ltd v Waterman Partnership Ltd* (2003), summarised in Chapter 4, in which the court questioned whether adjudication was appropriate for complex professional negligence disputes.

1.9 CONTRACTING OUT OF OR WAIVING THE RIGHT TO ADJUDICATE

The parties cannot contract out of the provisions of the Act and determination of the contract does not terminate the right to adjudicate.

Christiani & Nielsen Ltd v The Lowry Centre Development Company Ltd (2000)

Christiani were seeking to enforce the decision of an adjudicator that Lowry should pay £188,000, which had been deducted by them by way of liquidated damages.

Lowry had calculated the amount of liquidated damages to be deducted on the basis of a 57-week contract period even though the signed contract referred to an 81-week contract period. Lowry maintained that the reference to 81 weeks in the contract was a mistake common to both parties, which should therefore be rectified.

The adjudicator applied the terms of the contract as executed and ordered that the sums deducted by way of liquidated damages be paid to Christiani. Lowry refused to comply with this order so Christiani sought to enforce the decision of the adjudicator and applied for summary judgment.

Lowry raised a number of defences to the enforcement proceedings:

(1) They argued that the adjudicator sought to decide on his own jurisdiction when he had no jurisdiction to do so.

(2) They argued that although the contract was executed after 1 May 1998 it was in reality confirmation, as the contract had been created before that date. Therefore the Act did not apply.

(3) They argued that the parties had agreed that the contract would take effect from 11 August 1997 and that this agreement was made with the express intention of confirming that the Act would not apply to the executed contract.

(4) They argued that the real issue between the parties was whether or not the deed should be rectified, that in coming to his decision the adjudicator had decided on this question and that these issues were outside of his jurisdiction. As a consequence Lowry argued that the adjudicator's decision was a nullity.

With regard to the first point the court held:

> 'It has to be borne in mind when considering whether the parties did reach such an agreement that an adjudicator, faced with a challenge to his own jurisdiction, has a choice as to how to proceed. The adjudicator has three options:
>
> 1. He can ignore the challenge and proceed as if he had jurisdiction, leaving it to the court to determine that question if and when his decision is the subject of enforcement proceedings.
> 2. Alternatively, the adjudicator can investigate the question of his own jurisdiction and can reach his own conclusion as to it. If he was to conclude that he had jurisdiction, he could then proceed to decide the dispute that had been referred to him. That decision on the merits could then be challengeable by the aggrieved party on the grounds that it was made without jurisdiction if the adjudicator's decision on the merits was the subject of enforcement proceedings.

3. Having investigated the question, the adjudicator might conclude that he had no jurisdiction. The adjudicator would then decline to act further and the disappointed party could test that conclusion by seeking from the court a speedy trial to determine its right to an adjudication and the validity of the appointment of the adjudicator.

It is clearly prudent, indeed desirable, for an adjudicator faced with a jurisdictional challenge which is not a frivolous one to investigate his own jurisdiction and to reach his own non-binding conclusion as to that challenge. An adjudicator would find it hard to comply with the statutory duty of impartiality if he or she ignored such a challenge.'

The court concluded in this case that the parties had not consented to conferring ad hoc jurisdiction on the adjudicator to decide his own jurisdiction and that therefore this was a matter for determination by the court.

With regard to the second point, drawing from an interpretation of the words used in the letter of intent and in the deed itself, the court concluded that the deed superseded the earlier letter of intent and was not merely an agreement to vary the contract made in a letter of intent. Therefore the contract set out in the deed was made after 1 May 1998.

With regard to the third point, the court found against Lowry for two reasons. Firstly, the court decided that the legal basis now being advanced by Lowry (namely an argument based on estoppel) was not one that had been raised before the adjudicator and therefore Lowry should be prevented from making that argument now even though they had previously contested the jurisdiction of the adjudicator on different legal bases. Secondly, the court decided that Lowry's contentions should fail on the basis that any agreement or understanding of the parties that the Act would not apply, even though the contract had been entered into after 1 May 1998, would be one which robbed one of the parties of its statutory entitlement to an adjudication. Therefore the court concluded that parties cannot contract out of the adjudication provisions of the Act.

With regard to the fourth point, the court concluded that Lowry's claim for rectification would fail and that therefore the adjudicator had full jurisdiction to decide the dispute in the way that he did.

The court expressly made no decision on whether or not an adjudicator has jurisdiction to decide a claim for rectification.

Herschel Engineering Ltd v Breen Property Ltd (2000)

Herschel had referred a dispute to adjudication, notwithstanding that court proceedings had already commenced in respect of that same dispute. Breen refused to partake in the adjudication and failed to pay against the decision of the adjudicator.

Herschel sought to enforce the adjudicator's decision and applied for summary judgment. Breen resisted the application for summary judgment on the basis that by partaking in the court proceedings, Herschel had waived their rights to commence adjudication. The judge decided that there was no obvious reason why parliament should have intended to draw a distinction between cases where litigation or arbitration proceedings have been started before a dispute is referred to an adjudicator, and those where the proceedings have been started only after an adjudication has been completed. The judge concluded that parliament had decided that a reference to adjudication may be made at any time, and that there was no reason not to give those words their plain and natural meaning.

Further, the judge concluded that adjudication and litigation are not mutually exclusive routes to dispute resolution. Therefore, by commencing or partaking in litigation, a party cannot be said to have waived its rights to adjudication.

Joseph Finney plc v Vickers and another t/a Mill Hotel (a firm) (2001)

The court heard evidence that during the course of negotiations relating to a dispute over payment the parties had reached a compromise agreement, one of the conditions of which being that Finney would not pursue its threat to commence adjudication.

The court held in relation to this compromise agreement that:

> 'An exchange of mutual promises is good consideration. The promise not to adjudicate is a promise of value. An adjudication would involve expenditure of resource in terms of time, money and personnel and while the parties considered themselves as bound by the contract to compromise, the claimant could not have pursued an adjudication ...'

[This decision must be considered in the context of *Christiani & Nielsen Ltd v The Lowry Centre Development Company Ltd* (2000), in which the court held that the parties cannot contract out of the right of adjudication. However, unlike that case, the contract in this case arose after the parties were aware of the dispute.]

See also *Harwood Construction Ltd v Lantrode Ltd* (2000), summarised at 11.3 , in which Lantrode sought to resist the enforcement of an adjudicator's decision on the basis that there was on-going litigation between the parties. The judge dismissed this defence on the basis that adjudication is intended to determine the dispute on an interim and temporary basis pending resolution in other proceedings by litigation or arbitration.

1.10 THE EFFECT OF TERMINATION ON THE ENFORCEMENT OF AN ADJUDICATOR'S DECISION

Note that a number of cases in relation to this issue have come to different conclusions.

A & D Maintenance and Construction Ltd v Pagehurst Construction Services Ltd (2000)

A & D were appointed by Pagehurst as subcontractors in respect of extension works being undertaken at a school. Part of the works being undertaken by A & D included the installation of a boiler and flue. Disputes arose as to whether or not A & D's and therefore Pagehurst's works were complete, which eventually resulted in the school terminating Pagehurst's contract on 19 November 1998. On the same day, Pagehurst terminated A & D's contract.

On 27 November 1998 the school prepared a schedule of outstanding works. On 28 November 1998 a fire occurred at the school causing considerable damage to the extension and the main building. The loss adjusters for the school reported on 28 December 1998 that the cause of the fire was the negligent installation of the boiler.

A & D commenced adjudication proceedings against Pagehurst in respect of invoices that had not been paid, and obtained a decision from the adjudicator on 8 March 1999 that Pagehurst should pay them the sum of £103,665.80. These proceedings arose as a result of A & D seeking to enforce the decision of the adjudicator.

Pagehurst defended the enforcement proceedings on the following grounds:

(1) They argued that termination of the contract resulted in a termination of the implied terms including the right to adjudicate.
(2) They argued that some of the invoices that the adjudicator had ordered should be paid had not become payable under the timetable laid down in the Scheme.
(3) They argued that as there were other ongoing proceedings to recover the losses sustained by reason of the fire, the application for summary judgment to enforce the adjudicator's decision should be dismissed.

With regard to point (1), the court concluded that disputes referred to the adjudicator remain disputes under the contract notwithstanding termination of that contract. Where there is a contract to which the Act applies, as in this case, and there are disputes arising out of the contract to be adjudicated, the adjudication provision clearly remains operative just as much as an arbitration clause would remain operative.

With regard to point (2), the court concluded that the adjudicator had jurisdiction to consider the issues raised as to the payment of the invoices and that the correctness of his decision is not a matter that falls to be considered by the court when considering the limited issue of the enforceability of the adjudicator's decision.

With regard to point (3), the court concluded that it would not have been disposed to give leave to defend the enforcement proceedings in the absence of other proceedings. Further, that adjudication is a remarkable and possibly unique intervention whereby the ordinary freedom of contract between commercial parties to regulate their relationships has been overridden and that the intention of parliament is clear – that disputes are to go to adjudication and the decision of the adjudicator has to be complied with, pending final determination.

Therefore the court gave summary judgment for the claimant against the defendant.

Ferson Contractors Ltd v Levolux A T Ltd (2003), CA

This was a Court of Appeal decision following summary judgment to enforce the decision of an adjudicator to the effect that additional sums were payable to Levolux (a subcontractor to Ferson).

Ferson appealed a decision of the first instance court that summary judgment should be given enforcing the adjudicator's decision. Ferson were appealing on the basis that the subcontract had been terminated. Therefore, pursuant to the terms of the subcontract, 'all sums of money that may be due or accruing due from the contractor to the subcontractor will cease to be due or to accrue due'.

The Court of Appeal found that the contract must be construed so as to give effect to the intention of parliament rather than to defeat it. If that cannot be achieved by way of construction, then the offending clause must be struck down. The court suggested that in this case the intentions of parliament could be given effect without the need to strike out any particular clause, and that is by the means of reading the clauses (set out above) as not applying to monies due by reason of an adjudicator's decision.

Connex South Eastern Ltd v MJ Building Services Group plc (2005), CA

MJ Building Services Group (MJBSG) contracted with Connex for the installation of CCTV systems at various railway stations.

A single contract was entered into between MJBSG, Connex South Eastern Ltd and Connex South Central Ltd because the two Connex companies operated stations in different geographical regions. The contract consisted of a tender proposal dated 31 July 2000, which was accepted on behalf of the two Connex companies by their appointed project managers.

In August 2001 Connex South Central Ltd was acquired by another company and in December 2001 MJBSG were instructed not to commence any further installations until further notice.

In February 2002 Connex South Central Ltd agreed terms with MJBSG for the completion of specified works although Connex South Eastern Ltd continued to assert that there was no concluded contract between them and MJBSG.

In November 2002 MJBSG wrote to Connex South Eastern Ltd stating that its denial of the existence of a contract (and therefore of its liability to pay) was a repudiatory breach of contract, which MJBSG accepted, thereby terminating the contract.

In February 2004 MJBSG commenced adjudication proceedings against both Connex companies, which were stayed by consent pending the outcome of proceedings brought by Connex South Eastern Ltd seeking the following declaratory relief:

(1) That the agreement alleged in the notice of adjudication was not one whose material terms are recorded in writing as required by the Act.
(2) That following termination of the contract MJBSG no longer has any statutory right to adjudication.

(3) That MJBSG's notice of adjudication is an abuse of process because MJBSG were seeking to start adjudication proceedings so long after it purported in November 2002 to accept a repudiation of the contract by Connex South Eastern Ltd.

The court of first instance found that there was sufficient evidence in writing of the material terms of the agreement alleged in the notice of adjudication, that there was still a right to refer a dispute to adjudication notwithstanding the termination of the contract and that such a referral was not an abuse of process.

On appeal, the parties did not seek to challenge the decision of the judge in relation to points (1) and (2).

In relation to point (3), the Court of Appeal found that a party is entitled to refer the dispute to adjudication at any time, that this means exactly what it says, that therefore there is no time limit and that therefore the referral was not an abuse of process.

1.11 ADJUDICATING THE SAME DISPUTE TWICE

The same dispute cannot be adjudicated twice.

Sherwood & Casson Ltd v Mackenzie (1999)

Sherwood were subcontractors for the provision of steelwork and cladding; McKenzie were the main contractors. In a dispute between the parties the adjudicator had decided that Mackenzie should pay Sherwood a sum of money that totalled £12,803.14.

During enforcement proceedings it was argued that the adjudicator's decision related to substantially the same dispute that had been referred for determination by an adjudicator previously.

The judge concluded that the Scheme's wording was perfectly clear – namely that if the two disputes are substantially the same, the adjudicator must resign. This was a matter as to the adjudicator's jurisdiction, which must be determined by the court. The inquiry undertaken by the court should be conducted for the limited purpose of ascertaining whether or not two separate disputes are substantially the same. The court is not concerned to investigate the merits of the dispute, let alone resolve them.

In determining whether the two disputes were substantially the same, the judge was referred to the fact that the first dispute related to an interim valuation whereas the second dispute related to the valuation of the final account. The judge concluded that the two disputes were clearly different and refused to be drawn into any further consideration as to whether or not the adjudicator had made the right decision.

Holt Insulation Ltd v Colt International Ltd (2001)

This action arose out of two adjudication proceedings in relation to an interim application for payment (interim application number 10). In the first adjudication, Colt had claimed in the referral the sum of £110,587.56 plus interest. In that adjudication Holt had asserted and the adjudicator had agreed that his jurisdiction was limited to deciding whether or not that sum was due and therefore he did not have power to venture into deciding matters of alternative valuation. He concluded that the sum claimed was not due.

In the second adjudication Colt slightly amended its figures and claimed the sum of £97,309.77 or alternatively such other sum or sums as the adjudicator shall decide to be fair and reasonable in the circumstance plus interest.

Colt were successful in the second adjudication, the adjudicator deciding that the Holt were liable to pay £72,939.56, which Colt sought to enforce by way of commencement of insolvency proceedings. During the course of defending those insolvency proceedings Holt brought this application for a declaration that the second adjudication was invalid as it related to substantially the same dispute as the first adjudication.

The adjudications were being run pursuant to the Scheme for Construction Contracts, which provides that the adjudicator must resign where the dispute is the same or substantially the same as one which had previously been referred to adjudication and a decision has been taken in that adjudication.

The judge concluded that whilst the references to the adjudicator may have related to the same matters arising out of contractual relations between the parties they did not relate to the same dispute. There was nothing similar in the disputes; they were about different things. They may have been about the entitlement to claim in respect of the same work but the notices of referral were crucially different and in the judge's view the adjudicator was correct in reaching the decision that he did.

Skanska Construction UK Ltd v The ERDC Group Ltd and John Hunter (2002)

ERDC were appointed as a subcontractor to Skanska for the completion of various landscaping works. In December 2001 an adjudication took place in relation to an interim valuation and specifically in relation to ERDC's entitlement to loss and expense in the sum of £389,500.59. In that adjudication the adjudicator decided that Skanska were liable to pay nothing, on the basis that there was insufficient information, insufficient specification and insufficient evidence.

In September 2002 ERDC commenced a second adjudication in relation to their entitlement pursuant to the final account and in particular in relation to ERDC's entitlement to loss and expense in the sum of £372,978.35.

Skanska brought this application before the court during the currency of the second adjudication on the basis that the matter before the second adjudicator was substantially the same as the disputes that had been referred to and decided by the first adjudicator.

ERDC responded that the fact that this second referral arose pursuant to the final account was enough to make it a different dispute from that referred pursuant to an interim application. Further, ERDC asserted that this second referral contained a considerable amount of additional information that had not been available to the adjudicator in the first adjudication and that also made this a different dispute from the one previously referred.

The court concluded that the referral to the second adjudicator was not substantially the same as the dispute referred to the first adjudicator. A different stage in the contract had been reached; different contractual provisions applied; considerably more information may be available by the date of issue of the final account; and different considerations and perspectives may apply. The fundamental nature and parameters of the disputes are different.

Emcor Drake & Scull Ltd v Costain Construction Ltd & Skanska Central Europe AB (t/a Costain Skanska Joint Venture) (2004)

This case concerns the refurbishment of the Great Western Hotel at Paddington Station in London. The Costain Skanska Joint Venture (CSJV) were the main contractors and Emcor Drake & Scull were subcontractors. During the course of the works, Emcor made three claims for an extension of time – each one encompassing the previous one. The first claim was referred to adjudication in which Emcor failed to secure the extension of time claimed on the basis that they had failed to discharge the burden of proof. Importantly, the first adjudicator did not decide that Emcor were not entitled to the extension of time claimed, just that they had failed to prove that they were. The second claim was referred to adjudication separately in which Emcor were successful. Emcor sought to enforce this decision, which was resisted by CSJV on two grounds:

(1) CSJV argued that a significant part of the dispute referred to the second adjudicator had already been determined in the first adjudication and therefore the second adjudicator had no jurisdiction to reconsider these matters.
(2) CSJV argued that Emcor had submitted approximately 5,000 pages of information in its referral, to which it was unfair and an abuse of the adjudication process to require CSJV to respond in the second adjudication.

With regard to point (1), the judge found as a matter of fact that the second adjudicator had not trespassed on the first adjudicator's decision. However, the fact that the second adjudicator had considered the facts and matters considered by the first adjudicator in reaching his decision was not objectionable. It is interesting to note that the parties, the second adjudicator and counsel all considered the second adjudicator to be bound by the decision of the first.

In relation to point (2), the judge decided that the necessity to respond quickly to vast quantities of paperwork is one of the well known hazards of the adjudication process. That cannot of itself be a ground for contending that there has been an abuse of process.

1.12 THE HUMAN RIGHTS ACT 1998

The *Human Rights Act* 1998 does not apply to adjudication.

Austin Hall Building Ltd v Buckland Securities Ltd (2001)

This was the first case before the court in which it was said that the system of adjudication itself is unfair and offends against the European Convention on Human Rights – made legally effective in the UK by way of the *Human Rights Act* 1998. No allegation of unfairness was made against the adjudicator, nor was it alleged that the adjudicator did or omitted anything that reflected on his personal conduct.

The adjudicator had decided that Austin Hall should be paid £81,928.14 with interest and that Buckland should pay his fees.

This action was brought by way of an application for summary judgment to enforce the adjudicator's decision. The defendant alleged that it was denied its right to a fair trial guaranteed under article 6 of the European Convention on Human Rights and therefore the adjudicator's decision was a nullity and should be set aside. In particular, in the determination of the defendant's rights and obligations in the adjudication, the defendant was denied:

(1) a proper and equal opportunity to present its case to the claimant's final account;

(2) a reasonable time within which to respond to the claimant's final account.

Further, the defendant complained that it was not given a public hearing and that the decision was not pronounced publicly.

Article 6(1) of the European Convention on Human Rights is in the following terms:

> 'In the determination of his civil rights and obligations or of any criminal charge against him, everyone is entitled to a fair and public hearing within a reasonable time by an independent and impartial tribunal established by law. Judgment shall be pronounced publicly but the press and public may be excluded from all or part of the trial in the interests of morals, public order or national security in a democratic society, where the interests of juveniles or the protection of the private life of the parties so require, or to the extent strictly necessary in the opinion of the court in special circumstances where publicity would prejudice the interests of justice.'

The European Convention on Human Rights is incorporated into English law by means of the *Human Rights Act* 1998, section 6 of which provides that it is unlawful for a public authority to act in a way that is incompatible with a Convention right. However, this is subject to a number of provisos including if, as the result of one or more provisions of primary legislation, the authority could not have acted differently.

In this case the court relied on that proviso to dismiss the defendant's arguments that the time limits set by the adjudicator denied the defendant a proper and equal opportunity to present its case and a reasonable time within which to respond to the final account. In other words, the adjudicator was acting within the timetable dictated by the *Housing Grants, Construction and Regeneration Act* 1996 and could not have acted differently.

With regard to the right to a public hearing and the right to have the judgment publicly pronounced, the court was required to consider whether or not the adjudicator was a public authority within the terms of section 6 of the *Human Rights Act* 1998. Comparing the situation as it affects arbitrators, the court noted that arbitrators acting where the parties have consented to their dispute being resolved by arbitration do not come within the provisions of section 6, but those where the parties are required to have their dispute resolved by arbitration do come within the terms of section 6. However, even in this latter case, the court noted that the parties can consent to a waiver of the right to a public hearing.

The court, however, concluded that adjudicators make decisions, not judgments. The decision of an adjudicator is not enforceable of itself. Those decisions can be relied on as the basis for an application to the court for judgment, but they are not in themselves enforceable.

The court conceded that the arguments were finely balanced, but concluded that an adjudicator is not a public authority and is not bound by the *Human Rights Act* 1998.

In view of the fact that the arguments were finely balanced, the judge went on to consider the consequences of his decision being incorrect. He found that, in any event, the claimant's application should fail for the following reasons:

(1) If one considers the whole process necessary to enforce the adjudicators decision, then there is necessarily a public hearing before the decision is enforced (court proceedings), and therefore all the other requirements of article 6 of the Convention are satisfied.

(2) If there is a breach with regard to publicity, the *Human Rights Act* 1998 provides that the defendant can only rely on the Convention rights in legal proceedings if he is (or would be) a victim of the unlawful act. So far as lack of publicity goes, the court concluded that the defendant was not a 'victim'.

(3) The claimant had in any event waived his entitlement, if any, to a public or private hearing by failing to ask for a hearing.

1.13 COMPLEX DISPUTES

Some parties have argued that there are some cases that are simply too complex for adjudication.

CIB Properties Ltd v Birse Construction (2004)

This matter involved an adjudication where the dispute amounted to several million pounds. Mr John Uff QC was appointed as the adjudicator and he decided that Birse should pay CIB more than £2m. CIB sought to enforce this decision via summary judgment, and that was resisted by Birse on several grounds. Birse argued:

(1) The dispute had not crystallised at the time that the notice of intention to adjudicate had been served.

(2) CIB's tactics before the notice of the adjudication was served had put Birse at a disadvantage that could not be cured.

(3) The time pressures imposed on both Birse and the adjudicator had led the adjudicator to act unfairly and to the prejudice of Birse.

(4) The adjudicator made a slip in his award that transformed what should have been an award in Birse's favour into the present award in the favour of CIB.

(5) The size and complexity of the dispute meant that it could not be resolved fairly by adjudication.

With regard to point (1), the court found that the test is whether, taking a common sense approach, the dispute has crystallised. Even after it has crystallised, parties may wish to have further discussions in order to resolve it. Whether or not a dispute has, in fact, crystallised will depend on the facts in each case including whether or not the parties are in continuing and genuine discussions in order to try to resolve the dispute. The court found as a matter of fact that in the 15 intervening weeks between the notification of the claim and the date of the referral to adjudication there had been a proper opportunity for Birse to consider the claim and provide a constructive response, which may or may not have led to further discussions. Instead, Birse attempted to manoeuvre tactically so that it could make the claim that the dispute had not crystallised. Both sides had, for a long time before the start of the adjudication, been engaged in tactical manoeuvres. Looking at the history it is impossible to conclude that Birse was ambushed by CIB.

With regard to point (2), the court concluded that the conduct of CIB before the notice of adjudication did not render the whole process unfair or put Birse at an overwhelming disadvantage. It is clear that this was a very complex dispute and that Birse would require more than the 30 days originally stipulated in which to consider the claim. There was a 15-week period in which Birse could have made a constructive response. CIB at all stages carefully reserved its legal rights. Birse was aware, although CIB did not make it explicit, that this included the likelihood of a referral to adjudication of part or all of the claim. At an earlier stage Birse itself had sprung an adjudication on CIB.

With regard to point (3), the court concluded that the tests that the adjudicator set himself – namely that he could only reach a decision if (a) he had sufficiently appreciated the nature of any issue referred to him before giving a decision on that issue, including the submissions of each party; and (b) he was satisfied that he could do broad justice between the parties – were impeccable.

With regard to point (4), the court concluded that the law before this case is that in relation to a slip or alleged slip there are two questions: (a) Is the adjudicator prepared to acknowledge that he has made a mistake and correct it? (b) Is the mistake a genuine slip, which failed to give effect to his first thoughts? If the answer to both questions is 'Yes' then (subject to the important question of the time within which the correction is made and questions of prejudice) the court can, if the justice of the case so requires, give effect to the amendment to rectify the slip. If the adjudicator is not prepared to make a correction promptly, that is an end of the matter.

With regard to point (5), the court decided that there is a duty on the adjudicator to reach a decision provided that the conditions in section 108(2) of the Act are met. This means that the adjudicator must be able to discharge his duty to reach a decision impartially and fairly within the time limit stipulated in section 108(2)(c) and (d) of the Act. A defendant is not bound to agree to extend time beyond the time limits laid down in the Act even if such a refusal renders the task of the adjudicator to be impossible.

On the basis of the above reasoning, the adjudicator's decision was enforced.

See also *London & Amsterdam Properties Ltd v Waterman Partnership Ltd* (2003), summarised in Chapter 4, in which the court accepted that by the letter of the law complex professional negligence disputes could be adjudicated upon, but questioned whether adjudication was appropriate in such cases and therefore whether the Act needed to be reviewed.

2
The adjudication agreement

2.1 CONTRACT SCHEMES AND COMPLIANCE WITH THE ACT

The parties to a contract can agree on an adjudication procedure that, provided that it complies with the provisions of the *Housing Grants, Construction and Regeneration Act* 1996, will operate in lieu of the relevant Statutory Instruments, which are collectively referred to as the Scheme for Construction Contracts (hereafter referred to as 'the Scheme'). If the procedure agreed in the contract fails to comply with any of the provisions of section 108(2) of the Act, then the whole of the procedures set out in the Scheme will apply – not just those relating to the noncompliant parts of the procedures agreed in the contract.

2.2 THE NEC AND ICE CONTRACT SCHEME

John Mowlem & Co plc v Hydra-Tight Ltd (2000)

Hydra-Tight purported to refer a dispute in relation to their entitlement to payment to adjudication. Mowlem made an application to the court for a declaration that the adjudicator did not have jurisdiction.

The contract was the New Engineering Subcontract published by the Institution of Civil Engineers.

An issue arose as to whether the subcontract was compliant with the Act. The judge concluded that the subcontract was not compliant with the Act since the subcontract purported to defer the referral of a dispute to adjudication by four weeks pursuant to a mechanism by which the parties would first serve a notice of dissatisfaction.

Having reached this conclusion, it was necessary for the judge to consider whether, if some parts of the subcontract comply with the Act, they can be retained and the Act can be used in substitution for, or to fill in, those parts of the subcontract that are contrary to the Act. The judge concluded that the words of the Act are clear – either the parties comply in their own terms and conditions with the requirements of the Act or the provisions of the Scheme apply.

Provided that the procedure agreed in the contract complies with the provisions of section 108(2) of the Act, the parties may agree other supplementary provisions that can dramatically affect the costs or benefits of adjudication.

2.3 ONE PARTY PAYING THE OTHER PARTY'S COSTS

Bridgeway Construction Ltd v Tolent Construction Ltd (2000)

In this case the court decided that where the contract had been freely negotiated by the parties, a provision that required the referring party to pay the costs and expenses of any adjudication (including those of the adjudicator and responding party) was found to be enforceable. There were no public policy reasons as to why this provision should be declared void.

Deko Scotland Ltd v Edinburgh Royal Joint Venture and others (2003)

The dispute arose out of the construction of the new Edinburgh Royal Infirmary and Medical School. A company known as Zenith Contract Interiors Ltd was engaged as subcontractor to carry out plasterboard partitioning works. Subsequently a provisional liquidator was appointed to that company and the subcontract works were then novated from Zenith to Deko.

One of the clauses of that subcontract provided as follows:

> 'The Adjudicator may require any Party to pay or make contribution to, the legal costs of another Party arising in the Adjudication.'

Disputes arose between the parties, and an adjudicator was appointed. He decided that various sums were due to Deko by the Edinburgh Royal Joint Venture (ERJV).

In respect of the parties' costs, the adjudicator ordered that ERJV were liable for one-half of all Deko's costs of, and incidental to, the adjudication, including Deko's legal costs.

This action was brought by Deko claiming payment of the sums found due by the adjudicator and one-half of their expenses of the adjudication.

ERJV argued that Deko's claimed expenses should be confined to judicial expenses (i.e. those costs recoverable in a court action); and secondly that they should be subject to taxation. Further, ERJV argued that they should not be forced to pay the sums claimed until they had been taxed.

The court concluded that the clause referred to above confines the adjudicator to making an award of legal expenses and judicial expenses and that further, the award of expenses made by him is subject to taxation by the Auditor of Court.

Lomax Leisure Ltd v Fabric London Ltd (2003)

This was an action commenced by Lomax for a declaration that it was entitled to be indemnified by Fabric for claims arising out of a construction contract.

Lomax held a lease on a property and appointed a building contractor known as Marpaul to carry out construction works in relation to a development of that property.

Disputes arose between Lomax and Marpaul. Marpaul became insolvent and the building contract was terminated. Another contractor was then appointed to complete the works. Subsequently Lomax went into administration. As part of the disposal of Lomax's assets, the benefit of the lease and the building contract was sold to Fabric. The following clause was included in the contract of assignment:

> 'The Purchaser (Fabric) shall carry out and complete the Contracts with effect from the Transfer Date for its own account and shall keep the Vendor (Lomax) and the Administrator indemnified against all actions claims costs proceedings and demands in the extract of the Contracts and all the Assets or made against or

incurred by the Vendor and/or the Purchaser and/or the Administrator.'

Claims were made against Lomax by Marpaul, which Lomax sought to recover from Fabric under the terms of the above indemnity.

The judge concluded that the above clause did entitle Lomax to an indemnity for all actions, claims, costs, proceedings and demands 'made against the Vendor'. Therefore he gave the declaratory relief sought by Lomax.

2.4 ACTIONS OF THE PARTIES DURING THE COURSE OF THE ADJUDICATION

Whether or not the parties have agreed a procedure that complies with the provisions of section 108(2) of the Act, they can subsequently agree procedures that expand or deviate from the procedures previously agreed or as set out in the Scheme. This subsequent agreement can be by conduct, and parties unfamiliar with adjudication may therefore find themselves having agreed to a procedure that is detrimental to their position.

Nolan Davis Ltd v Steven P Catton (2000)

Disputes had arisen between the parties, which Nolan had referred to adjudication.

Mr Catton had argued before the adjudicator that he was not the correct contracting party but that it was instead one of his companies. The adjudicator had determined that Mr Catton was the correct contracting party and had proceeded to make a decision on that basis.

Nolan sought to enforce the decision of the adjudicator by way of an application for summary judgment, which Mr Catton sought to resist on the following grounds:

(1) There was no concluded contract between the parties.
(2) The adjudicator had decided on the allocation of costs between the parties when he had no jurisdiction to do so.

(3) Mr Catton sought a stay of execution of the summary judgment on grounds relating to his means.

With regard to point (1), the court concluded that the parties had agreed to be bound by the adjudicator's decision as to jurisdiction. Even though the arguments as formulated in these proceedings were not put to the adjudicator, the court was not prepared to revisit his decision.

With regard to point (2), the court concluded that both parties had applied for costs and had, thereby, conferred jurisdiction on the adjudicator to determine the allocation of costs between them. The court followed the decision in *Northern Developments (Cumbria) Ltd v J & J Nichol* (2000).

With regard to point (3), the court concluded that to grant a stay of execution on grounds relating to means would drive a coach and horses through the adjudication scheme, and would frustrate parliament's intention.

Whiteways Contractors (Sussex) Ltd v Impresa Castelli Construction Ltd (2000)

Whiteways were plastering subcontractors engaged by Impresa in connection with the construction of a hotel in London. Disputes arose, which were referred to adjudication. The adjudicator ordered that Impresa pay Whiteways the sum of £95,383.50 including VAT. These proceedings were brought by Whiteways and an application for summary judgment was made. Impresa resisted enforcement on the basis that the adjudicator had exceeded his jurisdiction by considering matters in the referral that were not referred to in the notice of adjudication.

On 3 March 2000, and in response to a referral served on 25 February 2000, Impresa issued the adjudicator with a document entitled 'Submission by Impresa Castelli Construction UK Limited on the matter of Jurisdiction'. The last paragraph of the covering letter read:

> 'We invite you to decide on this issue as a matter of urgency as our response to Whiteways' Notice of Referral will depend on your decision. Our client does

not wish to incur costs on matters which, in our view, fall outside the jurisdiction of the Adjudication.'

On the same day, the adjudicator invited Whiteways' solicitors to respond to the submission, which they did. The adjudicator subsequently, on 7 March 2000, wrote to the parties stating:

'… further to the submissions received from the parties I now attach my determination on the matter of my jurisdiction in this adjudication'.

The adjudicator decided that he did have jurisdiction to consider the matter referred (with one exception) and proceeded with the adjudication.

On 16 March 2000 the solicitors to the defendants served their response to the claimants' referral document. In that response the defendants repeated their objections to the jurisdiction and stated that the response was made without prejudice to that objection and reserved the right to raise the matter of jurisdiction in any future proceedings concerning this adjudication.

The judge concluded that the parties had given the adjudicator ad hoc jurisdiction to determine his own jurisdiction by their letters on or about 3 March 2000, and like the remainder of his decision his determination on his jurisdiction is binding on the parties until the dispute with difference is finally determined. The court saw no reason to differ from the finding of the adjudicator on jurisdiction, but in any event stated that the court is not a court of appeal from the adjudicator and therefore was not prepared to rehearse the adjudicator's reasons for making his decision on jurisdiction.

Having given the adjudicator ad hoc jurisdiction to determine his own jurisdiction and the adjudicator having acted on that, neither of the parties could unilaterally take that jurisdiction away.

Watson Building Services Ltd (2001)

This was a decision of the Scottish Courts in which Watson Building Services Ltd were seeking judicial review of the decision of an adjudicator.

Watson were the main contractors in respect of building work at a church in Glasgow. They appointed Miller Preservation Ltd as their subcontractors to undertake rot eradication works.

Miller sought to refer various disputes to adjudication. The subcontract did not of itself contain any adjudication provisions, but did incorporate, by reference, provisions from the main contract. The issue arose as to whether or not the adjudication provisions in the main contract had been properly incorporated by reference into the subcontract. Miller took the view that that they had not, that the subcontract was therefore not compliant with the Act and therefore formed the view that the Scheme for Construction Contracts applied. The appointment process that followed was compliant with the Scheme but not the adjudication provisions in the main contract.

The first adjudicator appointed formed the view that he did not have jurisdiction and therefore resigned. Miller sought the appointment of another adjudicator who took a different view and proceeded with the adjudication.

The decision of the second adjudicator was that Watson should pay Miller £7,917.35 plus VAT. Watson did not pay, so Miller raised an action for payment. Watson then commenced these proceedings for judicial review.

Watson contended that the adjudicator was not properly appointed because the contractual mechanism for making an appointment had not been followed. They further contended that, in any event, the adjudicator could only decide disputes arising under the contract and did not have jurisdiction to decide what formed the basis of the contract itself. In purporting to do so he was acting ultra vires.

Miller counter-argued that the question as to the incorporation of the main contract adjudication provisions into the subcontract was one that had been put before the adjudicator and was therefore a point which he had jurisdiction to decide. Having put that point before the adjudicator, the parties were bound by his decision even if it were wrong.

In this case the judge considered that the adjudicator had the power to determine the meaning and import of the subcontract terms, even where such an exercise resulted in his determining a dispute about the validity of his appointment and in effect his jurisdiction. Not only did he have the power and authority to carry out such an exercise, but a question relating to the proper construction of the subcontract terms, and thus the validity of his appointment, was expressly put to him by the parties. Accordingly, he was not answering a question that had not been put. The first respondent having had jurisdiction, and having acted within his jurisdiction, the petition in the judge's view falls to be refused.

The judge considered that Watson, by the explicit terms of their response, chose to place the issue of the proper construction of the terms of the subcontract, and thus the consequential matter of the correct procedure for the appointment of the adjudicator and the question of the adjudicator's jurisdiction and authority, before the adjudicator for his decision. In so doing, the judge considered that Watson unreservedly accepted that the dispute over the proper construction of the subcontract terms, insofar as relating to the appointment of the adjudicator, was to be treated, together with any other disputes (for example, about payment), as a 'dispute arising under the contract' which it was both competent and appropriate for the adjudicator to resolve – with all the consequences flowing therefrom.

The judge further concluded that, in any event, it was his opinion that the adjudication provisions in the main contract had not been effectively incorporated into the subcontract. Therefore the Scheme for Construction Contracts applied, and therefore the adjudicator had been properly appointed in any event.

Shimizu Europe Ltd v LBJ Fabrications Ltd (2003)

Shimizu appointed LBJ as subcontractors in relation to the design, supply and installation of louvres and cladding on a project for which Shimizu were main contractors. Disputes arose, which LBJ referred to adjudication. The adjudicator decided that Shimizu should pay LBJ the sum of £47,718.39 plus VAT without set-off.

Following receipt of this decision, LBJ issued an invoice against which Shimizu sought to set-off various sums. Shimizu then commenced these proceedings seeking declarations:

(1) that Shimizu are entitled to withhold the sums that they seek to set-off from the adjudicator's decision; and
(2) that the adjudicator reached his decision on the basis of a subcontract that the parties did not purport to exist whereas he should have reached his decision on the basis of the letter of intent. As such, the adjudicator's decision is a nullity and/or unenforceable.

The subcontract contained a provision making the issue of a VAT invoice a condition precedent to an entitlement to payment. Shimizu therefore argued that the sums did not fall due until after the VAT invoice had been issued and that they were entitled to issue a withholding notice in respect of those sums provided that they did so before the required time before the final date for payment.

LBJ counter-argued that the adjudicator's decision required Shimizu to pay the stated sum without set-off and that therefore Shimizu's attempts to withhold sums from the invoiced amount must fail.

The judge, considering the contractual mechanism for payment, concluded that the adjudicator did what Shimizu should have done, which was to value the work properly. The performance of that function, however, did not deprive Shimizu of its subsequent rights to withhold sums from the invoiced amount.

Although the letter of intent referred to the subcontract conditions, the important issue so far as this matter was concerned was that the letter of intent had a cap on liability that was lower than the sum that LBJ applied for and the sum that the adjudicator decided was the correct value of the works.

The judge decided that as a matter of fact the parties had in their submissions to the adjudicator agreed that their contractual relationship was governed by the terms of the letter of intent. Therefore the adjudicator did not have jurisdiction to decide otherwise. Insofar as the adjudicator purported to decide otherwise, he was acting outside of his jurisdiction and that part of his decision would be invalid.

See also *A. J. Brenton v Jack Palmer* (2001) and *Northern Developments (Cumbria) Ltd v J & J Nichol* (2000), summarised at 7.1.

2.5 CONTRACTS OUTSIDE THE SCOPE OF THE ACT

Even if the construction contract is one that is outside the scope of the Act, if the parties have included an adjudication procedure in their contract then the courts will enforce it.

Nordot Engineering Services Ltd v Siemens plc (2000)

Nordot were a subcontractor to Siemens in respect of the provision of mechanical works, pressure piping, assorted equipment and access platforms to machinery at Cottam Power Station. The work was associated with the provision of a gas turbine generating plant.

Disputes arose in relation to payment and in particular in relation to the applicability of a schedule of rates.

Nordot referred the disputes to adjudication and the adjudicator decided that Nordot should be paid additional sums in excess of £100,000 plus VAT.

These proceedings arose out of Nordot's application for summary judgment in relation to that decision.

Siemens argued before the adjudicator that he did not have jurisdiction to hear the matter because the subcontract was not one which fell within the scope of the Act, Nordot's responsibility being the erection and installation of plant and machinery, the primary activity on the site being power generation.

However, they went on to say to the adjudicator:

'We will, however, abide by your decision in this matter and will comply with whatever decision you deem appropriate. Should you require it we can furnish you with a detailed list of all activities that Nordot undertook at CDC Cottam which supports our above statements.'

The adjudicator concluded that the erection of access platforms formed part of the building structure and that he had jurisdiction to consider disputes arising in relation to this work.

Following this decision, Siemens responded to the referral, again raising the issue of the adjudicator's jurisdiction in the response.

The question facing the judge in the application for summary judgment was whether Siemens, by their actions, had conferred jurisdiction on the adjudicator to determine whether or not the contract with Nordot was within or outside the scope of the Act.

Siemens argued before the judge that the parties cannot contract into the Act, just as they cannot contract out of it, but this submission was dismissed by the judge who found that parties can, by agreement, confer jurisdiction on an adjudicator.

The judge concluded that Siemen's letter outlined above and sent to the adjudicator clearly conferred on the adjudicator ad hoc jurisdiction to determine the matter and that Siemens must therefore comply with his decision.

Construction contracts with residential occupiers are excluded from the provisions of Part II of the Act, and therefore there is no statutory right of adjudication. However, if an adjudication procedure is included in the construction contract, and provided that it does not fall foul of the provisions of the *Unfair Contract Terms Act* 1977, then it will be enforceable.

Gennaro Maurizio Picardi (t/a Picardi Architects) v Paolo Cuniberti (2002)

This action arose out of a claim by a firm of architects, Picardi Architects, against Mr and Mrs Cuniberti for fees for the refurbishment of their private dwelling house. This claim was referred to an adjudicator, who decided that Mr and Mrs Cuniberti should pay the outstanding sum of £42,862.19 plus VAT and the adjudicator's fees.

This action was brought by Picardi for a declaration (a) that the contract between the parties included the Construction Industry Council (CIC) model adjudication procedure; and (b) that the adjudicator's decision should be enforced.

It was agreed between the parties that if the contract between the parties does not include provisions relating to adjudication then there is no right to adjudicate, the contract being in relation to a dwelling house.

Cuniberti raised three defences to this action:

(1) There was no concluded contract with Picardi.
(2) If there was, insufficient notice was given of the specific and onerous obligations relating to adjudication.
(3) In any event, the clause should be declared of no effect by reason of the *Unfair Terms in Consumer Contracts Regulations* 1999 (SI 1999/2083) – the legal basis for which is Directive 93/13EEC on Unfair Terms in Consumer Contracts ('the Directive').

Picardi argued in relation to these three points:

(1) Their previous invoices had been paid pursuant to the contract – those invoices referring to the unsigned contract issued to Cuniberti.

(2) Adjudication was neither unusual nor onerous and therefore specific notice was not required.

(3) Adjudication does not hinder the right of either party to take legal action in court, or refer a matter to arbitration. Furthermore, they said that it does not act to the detriment of the consumer, since either party may refer the matter to adjudication.

With regard to point (1), the court concluded that there was no concluded contract between Picardi and Cuniberti that incorporated a right of adjudication. Therefore there was no right to adjudicate and therefore the purported decision of the adjudicator was invalid and unenforceable.

This decision alone was sufficient to dispose of the matter, but the court did go on to give guidance on the two remaining issues.

With regard to point (2), the court concluded that the inclusion of adjudication in consumer contracts that would otherwise be outside the scope of the Act was unusual and therefore did require the supplier to expressly bring such clauses to the attention of the consumer. Picardi had failed to do this, and therefore on this basis his application would have failed had it not failed under point (1) above.

With regard to point (3), the court further concluded that the introduction of adjudication would have introduced a significant imbalance in the parties' rights and obligations to the detriment of the consumer. Therefore if the claimant's application had not failed under points (1) or (2) above it would have failed under point (3).

In coming to this conclusion under point (3), the court was persuaded by the example given in the Directive of an arbitration clause that would give rise to such an imbalance; by the fact that the appointing body was the Royal Institute of British Architects (RIBA); and by the fact that the consumer was deliberately excluded by parliament from the scope of the Act.

Lovell Projects Ltd v Legg and Carver (2003)

Legg and Carver contracted with Lovell for the construction of a dwelling house pursuant to the JCT Minor Works 1998 ('JCT MW 98') standard form of building contract. Although the works were outside the scope of the Act, the proposed contract terms included adjudication within the dispute resolution provisions. An architect was also appointed.

At the time of tender, Lovell proposed alternative contract conditions but Legg and Carter were insistent that JCT MW 98 was used.

Disputes arose, which Lovell referred to adjudication. The adjudicator made his decision in terms that Legg and Carver should pay Lovell the sum of £85,873.59 plus VAT.

These proceedings were brought by way of an application for summary judgment to enforce that decision. Legg and Carver defended that application on the basis that the adjudication clause should be declared of no effect by reason of the *Unfair Terms in Consumer Contracts Regulations* 1999 (SI 1999/2083). Therefore the adjudicator's decision is a nullity.

The judge concluded that the JCT MW 98 terms do not exclude or hinder the consumer's right to take legal action or exercise any other legal remedy. On the contrary, an adjudication only binds the parties until the dispute or difference is resolved by legal action, arbitration or agreement (supplemental condition D7.1). The terms do not require the consumer to take disputes exclusively to arbitration. Nor do they restrict the evidence available to him or alter the burden of proof. In any case, Schedule 2 to the Regulations simply sets out a list of examples of terms that 'may' be regarded as unfair. In the judge's judgment the word 'may' does not confer any discretion, it simply introduces terms that may possibly qualify as unfair if the other requirements of regulation 5(1) are satisfied.

Further, the judge found that for the adjudication clause to be declared of no effect it was necessary to demonstrate that the clause caused a significant imbalance in the parties' rights and obligations under the contract to the detriment of the consumer. In view of the fact that the adjudication provisions could be applied either way, the judge was not convinced that the adjudication provisions created such a significant imbalance. Further, the judge found that there had been no breach of the requirement of openness and that the contractor did not either deliberately or unconsciously take advantage of the consumers' necessity indigence, lack of experience, unfamiliarity with the subject matter of the contract, weak bargaining position or any other factor listed in Schedule 2 to the Regulations.

The judge was referred to the decision in *Picardi v Cuniberti* but distinguished that case from this current case on the basis that the contractual terms were different: Cuniberti's dispute was with the architect who should have provided advice concerning the adjudication terms, and none of the relevant terms had been drawn to the client's attention, let alone specifically negotiated.

The judge therefore concluded that the employers in the present case were bound by the adjudication terms in their contract with the contractor and that they should therefore pay the full amount ordered by the adjudicator.

Bryen & Langley Ltd v Martin Rodney Boston (2004)

This was a matter involving an adjudicator's decision in favour of a contractor against a residential occupier. The decision of the court not to enforce the decision of the adjudicator was based on the conclusion that the JCT contract on which the contractor was relying had not been incorporated into the contract with the residential occupier. Nevertheless, the judge went on to consider the consequences of the alternative argument that, in any event, the adjudication procedure and the obligation to issue withholding notices were unfair and therefore could not be relied on as against consumers.

The judge concluded that in the majority of medium- to high-value construction projects involving consumers, the consumer will be advised by professional consultants and it will be the consumer acting on the advice of his consultants who invites tenders pursuant to the chosen contractual terms. In such cases, the judge concluded, it would be unlikely that the court would find that the chosen contractual terms were unfair to the consumer.

Further, the judge concluded that as long as the 'consumer' is aware of the requirement, and alert to the possible need to comply with it, it does not affect his rights at all. If the requirement is contained in a form of agreement that he has himself put forward, any ignorance on his part of the term is not likely to be as a result of the opposite party failing to act in good faith.

Westminster Building Company Ltd v Andrew Beckingham (2004)

This matter concerned the refurbishment of a property owned and occupied by Mr Beckingham as his residence. Specifications were prepared by a firm of chartered surveyors and the works were awarded to Westminster. It was common ground between the parties that the works were not subject to the provisions of the Act.

Westminster contended that the works were governed by the JCT Intermediate Form of Contract ('IFC'), which incorporated adjudication procedures. Beckingham denied this.

Disputes arose as to payment, which Westminster referred to adjudication following the procedures in the IFC form of contract. The adjudicator decided that Beckingham should pay Westminster the sum of £122,409.16 plus interest.

Those sums were not paid and these proceedings were brought by Westminster in which they applied for summary judgment in respect of the adjudicator's decision.

The enforcement proceedings were defended on three grounds:

(1) The contract did not include any adjudication provisions and therefore there was no right to adjudicate.
(2) Even if the contract had contained such provisions, the adjudication clause should be declared of no

effect by reason of the *Unfair Terms in Consumer Contracts Regulations* 1999 (SI 1999/2083). Therefore the adjudicator's decision is a nullity.

(3) Even if the above two arguments fail, the parties had agreed a maximum liability in respect of the works and the adjudicator had exceeded his jurisdiction by finding that a sum higher than this agreed cap was due and payable.

With regard to point (1), a letter of intent had been issued, which confirmed that formal contract documents would be issued for execution by the parties. Beckingham's surveyors had prepared such a document, which had been issued by Westminster, signed by Westminster and returned to Beckingham's surveyors. Beckingham's surveyors never indicated that there was any aspect of the contract with which they were unhappy, but the contracts were not sent to Beckingham for counter-signature.

The judge found as a matter of fact that a contract had come into being based on the IFC standard form of contract, notwithstanding that Beckingham had not counter-signed the contract.

With regard to point (3), the adjudicator had found that the agreement between the parties was unsupported by consideration and was therefore unenforceable. The judge refused to go behind the adjudicator's reasoning in this part of his decision, finding instead that the adjudicator had made a decision within his jurisdiction.

With regard to point (2), the judge was referred to the judgment in *Lovell v Legg and Carver* (2003) and concluded that:

'1. The terms in this case were not individually negotiated but were couched in plain and intelligible language.

2. The terms of the contract were decided upon by Mr Beckingham's agent, who are chartered surveyors, and Mr Beckingham had, or had available to him, competent and objective advice as to the existence and effect of the adjudication clause before he proffered and entered into the contract.

Westminster did no more than accept the contract terms offered and had no reasonable need to draw to Mr Beckingham's attention the potential pitfalls to be found in the adjudication clause and in its operation during the course of the work. The clause did not, therefore, contravene the requirement of good faith (see especially the speech of Lord Bingham in the *Director General of Fair Trading [v First National Bank plc* [2002] 1 AC 481] at page 494).

3. The clause did not, if considered at the time of making the contract, constitute a significant imbalance as to Mr Beckingham's rights (see especially the judgment of Judge Moseley [in *Lovell v Legg and Carver*] at paragraphs 28–29).

4. The clause does not significantly exclude or hinder the consumer's right to take legal action or other legal remedy or restrict the evidence available to him (see especially the judgment of Judge Moseley [in *Lovell v Legg and Carver*] at paragraph 27).'

For all these reasons, the judge concluded that the adjudication clause, on the facts of this case, was not unfair and was binding on Mr Beckingham.

3
Scheme adjudications

The scheme provided by section 108 of the *Housing Grants, Construction and Regeneration Act* 1996 was explained by Dyson J in *Macob Civil Engineering Ltd v Morrison Construction Ltd* (1999) at paragraph 14:

'The intention of Parliament in enacting the Act was plain. It was to introduce a speedy mechanism for settling disputes in construction contracts on a provisional interim basis, and requiring the decisions of adjudicators to be enforced pending the final determination of disputes by arbitration, litigation or agreement: see section 108(3) of the Act and paragraph 23(2) of Part 1 of the Scheme. The timetable for adjudications is very tight (see s 108 of the Act). Many would say unreasonably tight, and likely to result in injustice. Parliament must be taken to have been aware of this. So far as procedure is concerned, the adjudicator is given a fairly free hand. It is true (but hardly surprising) that he is required to act impartially (section 108(2)(e) of the Act and paragraph 12(a) of Part 1 of the Scheme). He is, however, permitted to take the initiative in ascertaining the facts and the law (section 108(2)(f) of the Act and paragraph 13 of Part 1 of the Scheme). He may, therefore, conduct an entirely inquisitorial process, or he may, as in the present case, invite representations from the parties. It is clear that Parliament intended that the adjudication should be conducted in a manner which those familiar with the grinding detail of the traditional approach to the resolution of construction disputes apparently find difficult to accept. But Parliament has not abolished arbitration and litigation of construction disputes. It has merely introduced an intervening provisional stage in the dispute resolution process. Crucially, it has made it clear that the decisions of adjudicators are binding and are to be complied with until the dispute is finally resolved.'

4
A dispute

Only matters that have crystallised into a dispute can be referred to adjudication.

Sindall Ltd v Solland and others (2001)

Sindall was a contractor to Solland.

Disputes arose with regard to Sindall's entitlement to an extension of time. Solland failed to give such an extension, which resulted in Sindall serving notice of suspension and notice of adjudication. The adjudication resulted in the adjudicator deciding that Sindall were entitled to a 28-week extension of time to 29 August 2000 and an additional sum of £462,222.51 plus VAT.

On 1 December 2000 Solland served notice of determination on Sindall for failing to proceed regularly and diligently.

On 21 December 2000 Solland determined Sindall's employment.

On 9 February 2001 Sindall sent to Solland three lever-arch files and supporting information in support of its claim for an extension of time and demanding a response within seven days.

On 15 February 2001 Solland responded that they needed more time.

On 16 February 2001 a notice of intention to adjudicate was served by Sindall. That notice sought a declaration that the determination was wrongful, and in the alternative that Sindall were entitled to a further extension of time and loss and expense.

The adjudicator decided that the determination was wrongful and that a further extension of time was due.

Sindall brought these proceedings to enforce the decision of the adjudicator. Solland resisted enforcement on the ground that at the time that the notice of intention to adjudicate was served on 15 or 16 February 2001, there was no dispute as insufficient time had elapsed since service of the files on 9 February 2001.

With regard to this point the judge concluded that for there to be a dispute for the purposes of exercising the statutory right to adjudication, it must be clear that a point has emerged in the process of discussion or negotiation which needs to be decided. At the time when the second adjudication as to extension of time was started, it was not yet clear that there was a dispute as to this because Sindall had not given Solland adequate time to respond in all the circumstances.

The notice of adjudication (assuming it to refer solely to the claim for an extension of time) was well meant, but, because of the letter of 9 February 2001, it was premature. Therefore the adjudicator had exceeded his jurisdiction by deciding on a matter that was not in dispute at the time of the notice.

Watkin Jones & Son Ltd v Lidl UK GmbH (2001)

Watkin Jones were a contractor who had been appointed by Lidl pursuant to the JCT 1998 Standard Form of Building Contract with Contractor's Design. This contract included a provision to the effect that the valuation applied for by the contractor must be a proper gross valuation for the purposes of interim payment as provided by clause 30.2A. The employer may then question it within five days by a notice as provided by clause 30.3.3. If that is done, the employer is only obliged to pay the amount which it does not question and which then becomes the amount due. The employer also has a further right, as provided by clause 30.3.4, within five days to specify an amount proposed to be withheld or deducted from the amount due, that is, the amount which the employer considers is the due amount under clause 30.3.3. Clause 30.3.5 says that where the employer does not give any notice pursuant to clause 30.3.3, the employer shall pay the contractor the sum included in the application for an interim payment.

Watkin Jones issued an application for interim payment in respect of which Lidl failed to issue a clause 30.3.3 notice. Watkin Jones therefore sought to be paid the sum applied for and in the first adjudication the adjudicator decided in favour of Watkin Jones's application.

Lidl then promptly commenced a second adjudication to determine the properly calculated sum which ought to have been applied for.

Watkin Jones then commenced court proceedings by way of a Part 8 claim for a declaration that the second adjudicator lacked jurisdiction to decide the matter referred. They argued that in the absence of a clause 30.3.3 notice it is not open to either party to go back over the sum applied for. The judge found these submissions to be correct and therefore gave the declaration sought, namely that the second adjudicator lacked jurisdiction to decide on the matter referred – there was no dispute.

Carillion Construction Ltd v Devonport Royal Dockyard Ltd (2002)

This matter arose out of a very complex series of facts relating to the construction of a nuclear submarine renovation dock at Devonport in Plymouth. Carillion were appointed by Devonport Royal Dockyard Ltd to undertake construction of the dock and for new buildings for a sum of £54m.

This agreement was overlaid by a target price and partnering arrangement whereby Carillion and Devonport would share the benefit of any underspend or the burden of any overspend.

During the course of the works, delays occurred and additional items were instructed such that three amendments to the contract were negotiated between the parties; in a further fourth amendment, Devonport sought to raise the target price to £98m, although this was rejected by Carillion who were arguing for £114m.

After the fourth amendment, Devonport issued two further amendments raising the target price to £105m.

The parties also negotiated a bonus payable to Carillion if they completed their works by February 2002. The purpose of this agreement was to enable a submarine to enter the dock for a re-fit. Although Carillion's works were not fully completed by February 2002, they were sufficiently complete to enable the submarine to enter the dock, and so Carillion claimed their entitlement to their bonus.

Disputes arose as to the true entitlement of Carillion, which Carillion referred to adjudication. The adjudicator decided that Carillion were entitled to a further sum of £7.5m in addition to sums already paid.

Devonport refused to pay the sums awarded by the adjudicator on the basis that the adjudicator's decision relied on an alleged oral agreement, and section 107 of the Act requires the construction contract to be in writing or evidenced in writing.

The judge concluded that the agreement was not evidenced in writing and therefore the adjudicator did not have jurisdiction to make the decision that he did.

Further, Devonport asserted that no dispute had arisen at the time that the matter was referred to adjudication. Devonport argued that Carillion first arguably asserted the claim that it advanced in the adjudication by letter received by Devonport on 9 July 2002. However, that claim did not expressly place reliance on the alleged oral contract. Devonport sought further clarification of this claim, which Carillion referred to adjudication on 6 August 2002 without providing the clarification sought.

The judge concluded that Devonport 'has not in fact been told and is unaware in what respects it is alleged to have broken his obligations'.

Therefore, enforcement of the adjudicator's decision failed because the adjudicator lacked jurisdiction both because he relied on an alleged oral contract and also because there was no dispute as to the matters referred at the time of the notice of intention to adjudicate.

Cowlin Construction Ltd v CFW Architects (2002)

Cowlin were appointed pursuant to a design and build contract for the rebuilding of servicemen's housing for the Ministry of Defence. CFW were appointed by Cowlin to undertake the design.

Disputes arose between Cowlin and CFW, which Cowlin referred to adjudication. The adjudicator decided that CFW should pay Cowlin the sum of £323,373.52 including VAT.

That sum remaining unpaid, these proceedings were brought by Cowlin, and an application was made for summary judgment to enforce the adjudicator's decision.

CFW defended these proceedings on the basis that the adjudicator had no jurisdiction. CFW based this argument on two grounds:

(1) CFW argued that there was no construction contract between the parties.
(2) CFW argued that there was no dispute capable of being referred to adjudication.

CFW's solicitors had initially proposed adjudication. Cowlin, accepting this invitation, and served notice of adjudication. During the course of that adjudication, CFW's solicitors had raised various jurisdictional challenges including the absence of a contract. Cowlin had also questioned the adjudicator's jurisdiction to address issues raised by a counter notice served by CFW.

In his decision, the adjudicator had set out the limit of his jurisdiction so far as he considered was agreed by the parties. This decision determined the basis of the contract upon which CFW and Cowlin were operating.

Subsequently Cowlin presented their financial claim, which was for the sum of £717,510.80. This was largely based on delay to the project, which Cowlin asserted was caused by CFW.

This claim was initially made by Cowlin on 27 February 2002. What was described as supporting documentation of the monetary claim was then supplied by Cowlin on 11 March 2002. CFW responded by asking for full details to demonstrate that they were liable for the costs.

On 4 April 2002 CFW wrote to Cowlin asking Cowlin to direct all future correspondence to their insurers.

On 12 April 2002 Cowlin wrote to CFW's insurance brokers, and on 24 April 2002 Cowlin wrote to CFW's insurance underwriters. At this time Cowlin also amended their claim by adding a further head of claim.

A meeting was held between Cowlin and loss adjusters for the underwriters on 1 May 2002.

On 3 May 2002 Cowlin wrote to the loss adjusters giving them until 17 May 2002 to make a satisfactory offer.

The loss adjusters responded on 14 May 2002, stating that in view of the various complexities of the allegations, a review of the files was taking longer than anticipated but that they would respond as soon as possible.

On 18 May 2002 Cowlin served their notice of intention to adjudicate and subsequently applied to the Royal Institute of British Architects (RIBA) for the appointment of an adjudicator.

The second adjudicator proceeded on the basis of the decision of the first adjudicator and decided that a sum of £323,373.52 should be paid to Cowlin forthwith.

The judge concluded that CFW initially accepted that the adjudicator had jurisdiction. They then changed their mind. The adjudicator ignored that jurisdictional objection.

The judge concluded that, having elected to affirm the adjudicator's jurisdiction and having expressly sought decisions by the adjudicator, and bearing in mind that CFW were at that time represented by solicitors, CFW waved its rights to object to the jurisdiction of the adjudicator. CFW could not go back on that election. Accordingly, the adjudicator had jurisdiction to decide on matters that he dealt with.

With regard to the crystallisation of the dispute, the judge reviewed the authorities and concluded that a dispute had arisen at the time of the second notice of adjudication. She concluded that by 1 May 2002 CFW had had sufficient details of Cowlin's claim for nearly eight weeks. From this information CFW should have known broadly whether they admitted some or all of Cowlin's claim or rejected it totally. Following the meeting with the loss adjusters on 1 May 2002, Cowlin afforded CFW a further two weeks for a substantive response. The judge concluded that Cowlin's demands could not be said to have been high-handed or unjustified. By the time the deadline of 17 May 2002 passed, there was undoubtedly a dispute.

Therefore, judgment was entered for Cowlin.

Edmund Nuttall Ltd v R G Carter Ltd (2002)

Nuttall were subcontractors to Carter in relation to the basement and substructure works of a new civic community centre and library in Norwich. Disputes arose as to entitlements for extensions of time and loss and expense, which Nuttall referred to adjudication. The adjudicator decided that Carter should pay Nuttall the sum of £1,023,115. Carter did not pay, arguing that a dispute had not arisen in respect of the matter referred and therefore the adjudicator had no jurisdiction to decide on the matter. The crux of Carter's complaint was that Nuttall had referred different issues from the ones that had formed the basis of prior exchanges between the parties.

Nuttall had formulated a claim for an extension of time and loss and expense, which they had sent to Carter in May 2001 (referred to as 'the May claim'). This claim amounted to a total sum claimed of £1,979,752. This claim was formally responded to by Carter on 23 August 2001, in which this claim was rejected.

After further exchanges of correspondence, Nuttall issued a notice of intention to adjudicate on 14 December 2001 in which they claimed (a corrected) sum of £1,253,495.76 or such other sum as the adjudicator may consider appropriate.

Attached to the referral notice was a claim for an extension of time based on a report prepared by Mr Anthony Caletka ('the Caletka report'). This report had not previously been disclosed to Carter. Whilst this report showed that Nuttall were entitled to the same extension of time that had been claimed in the May claim (235 days), the justification of the extension of time was quite different. The basis of the calculation for the entitlement to loss and expense was also quite different from the May claim.

Considering the judgments in *Fastrack v Morrison* (2000), *Sindall v Solland* (2001) and *K&D Construction v Midas Homes* (2001), the judge concluded that there was more to a dispute than simply a claim that has not been accepted. He concluded that for there to be a dispute, there must have been an opportunity for the protagonists each to consider the position adopted by the other and to formulate arguments of a reasoned kind. What constitutes a dispute between the parties is not only a claim that has been rejected, if that is what the dispute is about, but rather the whole package of arguments advanced and facts relied upon by each side. A party can refine its arguments and abandon points not thought to be meritorious without altering fundamentally the nature of the dispute between them. However, what a party cannot do is abandon wholesale facts previously relied on or arguments previously advanced and contend that because the claim remains the same as that made previously, the dispute is the same.

The judge concluded that the dispute that was referred to adjudication in the notice of adjudication was the dispute as set out in the May claim. In fact, the adjudicator had based his decision on the Caletka report, which did not form part of that dispute. Therefore, the adjudicator based his decision on something that had not been referred to him for decision; his decision was therefore made without jurisdiction and was therefore unenforceable.

Hitec Power Protection BV v MCI Worldcom Ltd (2002)

The claimants were suppliers of diesel generators. They entered into a framework agreement with the defendant whereby the defendant (or any of its nominated affiliates) could place orders pursuant to the agreed terms. Where affiliates were to place the orders, the defendant would act as their agent, and if payment by the affiliates was not forthcoming the defendant undertook to make payment on the provision of notice from the claimant.

Four purchase orders were given, three by affiliates and one by the defendant. Invoices were not paid in full, so the claimant sought to enforce payment against the defendant. The framework agreement included adjudication provisions and notice provisions.

Unfortunately, the means by which the various notices were served and the operation of deeming provisions in the framework agreement meant that the notices of adjudication were deemed to have arrived with the defendant before the notices demanding payment.

The judge ruled that in those cases, a dispute could not be said to have arisen between the claimant and the defendant at the time that the notices of intention to adjudicate were properly served. Therefore the adjudicator had no jurisdiction to decide that sums were due.

Further, the parties had agreed to combine all of the referrals into a single adjudication in respect of which the adjudicator made a single decision. It was argued that even if disputes in respect of the orders placed by the affiliates could not have arisen at the time that the notices of intention to adjudicate were served, the same could not be said of the order placed directly by the defendant. However, this argument also failed, as it would have required the judge in a summary judgment application to go behind the decision of the adjudicator and attempt to dissect it for the benefit of the enforcing party. This the judge was not prepared to do.

Beck Peppiatt Ltd v Norwest Holst Construction Ltd (2003)

Beck Peppiatt were subcontractors to Norwest Holst in relation to construction works at First Central Guinness headquarters. Disputes arose in relation to entitlements to extensions of time, the valuation of loss and expense and the final evaluation of the variation account.

Discussions in relation to these items had been ongoing for a considerable amount of time during 2002, culminating in a letter from the chairman of Beck Peppiatt to Norwest Holst setting out Beck Peppiatt's claims and stating that unless their account was settled at a minimum of £2,300,000 and 90 per cent of the balance of money owed to them was paid by the end of January 2003, they would commence adjudication.

On 29 January 2003 Norwest Holst served on Beck Peppiatt 11 lever-arch files of information. The covering letter to these lever-arch files stated that unless Beck Peppiatt agreed to the account by close of business on 12 February 2003, Norwest Holst would consider that the account is not agreed, that the two companies were in dispute and that adjudication would then be immediately commenced.

Beck Peppiatt responded to this letter stating that they needed longer than the period from 29 January 2003 to 12 February 2003 to consider the information contained within the files and that if Norwest Holst carried out their threat of commencing adjudication it would no doubt fail on the basis that the dispute has not crystallised.

Norwest Holst rejected Beck Peppiatt's stance and initiated the referral to adjudication on 17 February 2003.

These proceedings arose out of an application by Beck Peppiatt for a declaration by the court that the adjudicator did not have jurisdiction to decide the matters referred on the basis that a dispute had not crystallised at the time that the notice of intention to refer was served.

The judge concluded that a point was reached in February 2003 when the process of discussion and negotiation had ended and that something was needed to be decided, namely the correct position with regard to the outstanding items on the final account.

Therefore the judge refused to give the declaration requested and advised the parties to get on with the adjudication.

Costain Ltd v Wescol Steel Ltd (2003)

Wescol was a subcontractor to Costain. Disputes arose between the parties as to the amount of money due to Wescol for variations and to their entitlement to an extension of time. Wescol then went into administrative receivership and the receivers referred the dispute to adjudication.

During the course of that adjudication Costain applied to the court for a declaration that the adjudication process was invalid. In their application they relied on the following grounds:

(1) A dispute had not crystallised at the time that the notice of intention to adjudicate was issued because:
   (a) Costain had indicated that they were still looking into the matter; and
   (b) the final account had not fallen due for payment at the time that the notice of adjudication was issued.
(2) That the notice of intention to adjudicate refers to two disputes; namely the amount of the final account and whether an extension of time for delay should be granted.

In relation to point (1), the judge took a common sense approach and concluded that a dispute had arisen as to the value of the final account at the time the notice of intention to adjudicate was served. He based this part of his judgment on the fact that there was no further communication on either side between 7 November 2002 (when Costain indicated that they were looking into the matter) and 13 December 2002 (when the notice of intention to adjudicate was served). He also took into account the fact that Costain denied that the money was at present due. Therefore, he concluded that the adjudicator could proceed to make a decision on the value of the final account even if he could not decide that any money should be paid.

In relation to point (2), the judge concluded as a matter of fact that the matters referred constituted one dispute.

Dean and Dyball Construction Ltd v Kenneth Grubb Associates (2003)

D&D Construction were undertaking construction works associated with a new Marina for D&D Developments. As part of those works it was necessary to construct a marine gate. Grubb was a consulting engineer and was approached by D&D Construction to design the gate.

D&D considered that the gate as designed by Grubb did not operate properly. There followed a period during which various claims were made, followed ultimately by a notice of adjudication. However, although the notice of adjudication relied on the rehearsed arguments with regard to the failure of the gate and the negligence of Grubb, the sum claimed in the notice was different from any sum previously claimed in correspondence.

The adjudicator decided that Grubb were liable for the sum of £315,390.14. Grubb resisted enforcement of that decision on many grounds, one of which was that, relying on the decisions in *Nuttall v Carter* (2002), the matter referred had not formed part of the exchange of arguments between the parties.

The judge at the enforcement proceedings was the same judge who had decided the case of *Nuttall v Carter*, who held as follows:

> 'In my judgment whether, at the point of the giving of a notice of adjudication, there is a crystallised dispute in respect of the matter sought to be referred when the quantum of the sum claimed and the alleged composition of that sum has altered from the sum previously claimed is a question of fact and degree the answer to which depends upon what, on the facts, the dispute between the parties was actually about. If liability in respect of a claim is not, at the point of giving notice of adjudication, in dispute, so that the only dispute is about quantum, it is likely to be difficult

to say that there is a dispute about a formulation of quantum which is new at that stage and which the responding party has not had an opportunity to consider. However, as it seems to me, the situation is different if liability itself is in dispute and the party alleged to be liable has not accepted that it is bound to pay to the other party any sum whatever. In such a case there is a crystallised dispute as to liability – it is denied – and a crystallised dispute as to the obligation of the party alleged to be liable to make a payment to the other party – the responding party's position is that it will pay nothing. Those crystallised disputes do not cease to be crystallised simply because the quantum of the claim is altered.'

The judge was clearly troubled by the adjudication rules in the Association of Consulting Engineers (ACE) Conditions, which allow the adjudicator to take evidence from one party in the absence of the other. However, in this case he concluded that:

'There was no suggestion in the present case on behalf of Grubb that [the adjudicator] did in fact have regard to evidence given on behalf of D and D of which [Grubb] was unaware or which [Grubb] did not have an opportunity to answer. The objection was simply one of form. It involved the somewhat unpromising proposition that the Procedure, if operated in accordance with its express terms, could be operated unfairly. Perhaps that could happen, but I am satisfied that it did not happen in the present case and that no dispassionate observer, aware of the circumstances, would consider that there was a risk of actual unfairness on the part of [the adjudicator].'

London & Amsterdam Properties Ltd v Waterman Partnership Ltd (2003)

This action arose out of a claim for professional negligence. L&AP argued that Waterman (a firm of structural engineers) had caused them to incur additional costs of approximately £1.9m due to the late release of steelwork design information. This led to a substantial period of exchanges of arguments and information between the representatives of the parties, although this focused on liability. Very little information was exchanged as to the actual loss incurred by L&AP as a result of the alleged negligence.

An adjudicator was appointed, and as part of the referral to the adjudicator substantial additional information was provided in relation to quantum particulars.

The adjudicator decided that Waterman should pay L&AP the sum of £659,346.

Shortly after the decision of the adjudicator was made, Waterman applied to the courts for a declaration that the purported decision was not binding because the adjudicator did not have jurisdiction or had exceeded his jurisdiction.

Shortly after that application was made, L&AP made an application for summary judgment in the amount of the adjudication award plus the adjudicator's fee.

One argument raised by Waterman was that the contract required the referral notice to be restricted to 20 single sided A4 pages. In fact the referral exceeded 1000 pages. Waterman had objected to the size of the referral during the course of the adjudication and the adjudicator had admitted the first 20 pages as the referral and the balance under his jurisdiction to admit further information. The judge concluded that provided the first 20 pages sufficiently identified the dispute that existed the adjudicator was entitled to regard that as a reference compliant with the contract and the Scheme and thereafter to make directions to receive the additional documentation.

In relation to the quantum information provided during the course of the adjudication, the judge concluded that there was a dispute as to liability and that was sufficient to embrace both the liability and quantum aspects of this large and complex claim. However, in relation to the manner in which additional quantum information was admitted into the adjudication, the court found that the adjudicator had acted in breach of the rules of natural justice and therefore his decision was unenforceable.

The court held that the adjudicator did not appear to have appreciated that in accordance with the rules of natural justice, he should either have excluded late additional information, or should have given the other party a reasonable opportunity of dealing with it. Under the applicable rules the adjudicator was precluded from taking the latter course because L&AP declined to agree to the necessary extension of time; he should therefore have excluded the evidence. In fact, he avoided a decision as to whether or not the evidence should be admitted and then based his decision upon the additional evidence without giving the other party a proper opportunity to deal with it. That was held to be a substantial and relevant breach of natural justice.

It was also alleged that the adjudicator exceeded his jurisdiction by making errors on points of law in deciding that Waterman had been negligent when there was insufficient evidence before him to come to that conclusion; however, the court dismissed that challenge on the basis that if the adjudicator made a decision on the basis of a dispute properly referred, then the court does not have power to interfere with that finding. However, in coming to this conclusion the judge said that these disputes arose at the very end of the contract. A party seeking 'a provisionally final decision' in a complex case such as this and involving professional negligence clearly perceives an advantage in doing so. It is a practice within the letter of the law and within the Act. A review as to the working of the Act in practice is perhaps now timely.

Orange EBS Ltd v ABB Ltd (2003)

Orange were a subcontractor to ABB in connection with works at the John Radcliffe Hospital in Oxford. Disputes arose as to entitlement to payment, and subsequently Orange withdrew from the site on the basis that their works were completed.

By letter dated 6 July 2002 ABB purported to terminate Orange's subcontract on the basis that the works were not complete.

By letter dated 10 July 2002 Orange referred to the dispute that now existed between themselves and ABB.

By letter dated 2 December 2002 Orange denied that they had abandoned the site and contended that ABB had wrongfully denied them access to site and/or terminated the subcontract. Orange enclosed their final account, seeking a gross valuation of £270,417. Orange also included a formal notice of intention to refer the matter to adjudication.

By letter dated 12 December 2002 ABB's solicitors wrote to Orange's representative contending that there was no extant dispute between the parties at that stage capable of adjudication because ABB had not had an opportunity to consider Orange's final account. They said that ABB would have completed the review of the final account by 20 January 2003.

By letter dated 6 January 2003 Orange's representatives served a formal notice of intention to refer to adjudication claiming the same redress as in their notice to adjudicate dated 2 December 2002.

On 9 January 2003 an adjudicator was appointed and on 14 February 2003 he gave his first decision, concluding that ABB had wrongfully terminated Orange's subcontract. He gave his second and final decision on 4 March 2003. The adjudicator decided that Orange were entitled to a total sum of £90,283.77 plus VAT.

This application for summary judgment was brought by Orange by way of enforcement of the adjudicator's decision. The application was resisted by ABB on the ground that no dispute had arisen at the time that the notice of intention to adjudicate was served on 6 January 2003. Not only had ABB said that they would need until 20 January 2003 to review the final account, but the contractual mechanism allowed them time from submission of the subcontractor's final account to review that information and respond. That period had not expired, so no dispute had arisen.

The judge concluded that the termination of Orange's contract brought the final account process to an end.

Further, and notwithstanding the fact that ABB had said that they would have the response ready by 20 January 2003, the judge concluded that by 6 January 2003 sufficient time had elapsed for evaluation and discussion or negotiation of Orange's claim. He reached that conclusion notwithstanding that the holiday period intervened. The judge concluded that by 6 January 2003 the process of negotiation and discussion of Orange's claim had come to an end, so that a dispute then arose. Therefore, the adjudicator had jurisdiction to decide as he did and Orange were entitled to judgment.

R Durtnell & Sons Ltd v Kaduna Ltd (2003)

Durtnell were undertaking works for Kaduna pursuant to a JCT Standard Form of Building Contract. The scope and timing of the works was considerably increased, as a result of which disputes arose between the parties. Durtnell referred these disputes to adjudication and the adjudicator decided that Durtnell should be paid approximately £1.2m. However, Kaduna only paid about half of this sum, arguing that the adjudicator had exceeded his jurisdiction with regard to the remainder. Durtnell brought these proceedings for payment of the balance.

The grounds on which it was argued that the adjudicator lacked jurisdiction were:

(1) That no dispute had arisen in relation to the entitlement of Durtnell to an extension of time at the time that the notice of intention to adjudicate was issued. It was argued that the time allowed in the contract for the contract administrator to make a determination in respect of the application had not expired and that no determination had been made.

(2) It was argued that, on its strict interpretation, the notice of intention to adjudicate asked the adjudicator to decide as a matter of principle that the items listed were variations that caused the completion of the works to be delayed. The notice did not require the adjudicator to calculate how much delay was caused or the amount to which Durtnell was entitled by way of payment of loss and expense.

Further, it was argued on behalf of Durtnell that Kaduna could not accept part of the adjudicator's decision and challenge other parts of it: by a principle of law known as 'approbate or reprobate' it was argued that Kaduna must either accept or reject the entire decision. By paying pursuant to part of the decision it was argued that Kaduna had committed themselves to accepting the entire decision.

Further, it was also alleged that even if the adjudicator lacked jurisdiction, Kaduna had taken part in the adjudication and were now prevented from raising such arguments.

The judge compared the JCT adjudication scheme in clause 41a of the contract with the Scheme for Construction Contracts and concluded that whilst it was clear that under the Scheme for Construction Contracts only one dispute could be the subject of one notice of adjudication, the same did not apply to the JCT adjudication scheme.

With regard to the claim for an extension of time and loss and expense, the judge concluded that no dispute had arisen or could have arisen in relation to the extension of time until such time as the architect had made his determination or the contract period for the making of such determination had elapsed without a decision being made. This had not happened in this case, and therefore no dispute as to the extension of time entitlement had arisen at the time that the notice of intention to adjudicate was served.

The judge further concluded that, in any event, on a strict interpretation of the notice of intention to adjudicate, this issue was not one that has been referred to the adjudicator at all.

With regard to the application of the principle of approbation and reprobation, the judge concluded that this principle did apply to adjudication. However, in the current case, Durtnell had referred several disputes and it was open to them without falling foul of that principle to accept the adjudicator's decision in relation to some of those disputes whilst challenging it in relation to others.

With regard to Kaduna taking part in the adjudication, the judge concluded that the test to be applied is one of waiver.

That is to say, a party is not disabled from relying upon a point that an adjudicator has decided something not referred to him or not in dispute at the time of the notice of referral unless, with knowledge of the availability of the point, he has elected not to raise it. In the present case, the judge concluded that the courses that the adjudicator took that were not justified and that were in excess of jurisdiction were not such as Kaduna either did, or should have, appreciated, such that Kaduna's failure to raise the questions of jurisdiction any earlier should be treated as a waiver of the right to do so now.

The judge therefore concluded that Durtnell's arguments for payment of the balance of the sums decided by the adjudicator should fail.

Collins (Contractors) Ltd v Baltic Quay Management (1994) Ltd (2004), CA

The employer failed to issue withholding notices but sought to deduct sums from an interim application. The contractor sought to enforce these rights in court. The employer sought to have the court proceedings stayed on the basis of an arbitration agreement. The contractor argued that there was no real dispute as to the absence of withholding notices and therefore the application for the stay for arbitration should be refused.

In considering the meaning of 'dispute' the Court of Appeal adopted a seven-point test proposed by Jackson J in *AMEC Civil Engineering Ltd v The Secretary of State for Transport* (2004). That test was as follows:

> 'From this review of the authorities I derive the following seven propositions:
>
> 1. The word "dispute" which occurs in many arbitration clauses and also in section 108 of the Housing Grants Act should be given its normal meaning. It does not have some special or unusual meaning conferred upon it by lawyers.
> 2. Despite the simple meaning of the word "dispute", there has been much litigation over the years as to

whether or not disputes existed in particular situations. This litigation has not generated any hard-edged legal rules as to what is or is not a dispute. However, the accumulating judicial decisions have produced helpful guidance.

3. The mere fact that one party (whom I shall call "the claimant") notifies the other party (whom I shall call "the respondent") of a claim does not automatically and immediately give rise to a dispute. It is clear, both as a matter of language and from judicial decisions, that a dispute does not arise unless and until it emerges that the claim is not admitted.

4. The circumstances from which it may emerge that a claim is not admitted are Protean. For example, there may be an express rejection of the claim. There may be discussions between the parties from which objectively it is to be inferred that the claim is not admitted. The respondent may prevaricate, thus giving rise to the inference that he does not admit the claim. The respondent may simply remain silent for a period of time, thus giving rise to the same inference.

5. The period of time for which a respondent may remain silent before a dispute is to be inferred depends heavily upon the facts of the case and the contractual structure. Where the gist of the claim is well known and it is obviously controversial, a very short period of silence may suffice to give rise to this inference. Where the claim is notified to some agent of the respondent who has a legal duty to consider the claim independently and then give a considered response, a longer period of time may be required before it can be inferred that mere silence gives rise to a dispute.

6. If the claimant imposes upon the respondent a deadline for responding to the claim, that deadline does not have the automatic effect of curtailing what would otherwise be a reasonable time for responding. On the other hand, a stated deadline and the reasons for its imposition may be relevant factors when the court comes to consider what is a reasonable time for responding.

7. If the claim as presented by the claimant is so
nebulous and ill-defined that the respondent cannot
sensibly respond to it, neither silence by the
respondent nor even an express non-admission is
likely to give rise to a dispute for the purposes of
arbitration or adjudication.'

Carillion Construction Ltd v Devonport Royal Dockyard Ltd (2005)

This matter arose out of the same project as the previous
matter between the same parties, outlined above.

Following extended attempts to negotiate a resolution to the
disputes and one failed attempt at adjudication, a notice of
adjudication was served on 4 January 2005.

Following the various submissions of the parties during the
course of the adjudication, the adjudicator was served with
29 lever-arch files of material.

The adjudicator decided that Devonport should pay
Carillion the total sum of £10.6m plus VAT within seven
days.

Devonport refused to pay and Carillion referred the matter
to the courts. In the course of his judgment the judge restated
four basic principles:

'1. The adjudication procedure does not involve the
final determination of anybody's rights (unless all
parties so wish).
2. The Court of Appeal has repeatedly emphasised
that adjudicators' decisions must be enforced, even
if they result from errors of procedure, fact or law:
see *Bouygues*, *C&B Scene* and *Levolux*.
3. Where an adjudicator has acted in excess of his
jurisdiction or in serious breach of the rules of
natural justice, the court will not enforce his decision:
see *Discain*, *Balfour Beatty* and *Pegram Shopfitters*.
4. Judges must be astute to examine technical defences
with a degree of scepticism consonant with the
policy of the 1996 Act. Errors of law, fact or

procedure by an adjudicator must be examined critically before the Court accepts that such errors constitute an excess of jurisdiction or serious breaches of the rules of natural justice: see *Pegram Shopfitters* and *AMEC*.'

Having restated the four basic principles, the judge made five propositions:

'1. If an adjudicator declines to consider evidence which, on his analysis of the facts or the law, is irrelevant, that is neither (a) a breach of the rules of natural justice nor (b) a failure to consider relevant material which undermines his decision on *Wednesbury* grounds or for breach of paragraph 17 of the Scheme. If the adjudicator's analysis of the facts or the law was erroneous, it may follow that he ought to have considered the evidence in question. The possibility of such error is inherent in the adjudication system. It is not a ground for refusing to enforce the adjudicator's decision. I reach this conclusion on the basis of the Court of Appeal decisions mentioned earlier. This conclusion is also supported by the reasoning of Mr Justice Steyn in the context of arbitration in *Bill Biakh v Hyundai Corporation* [1988] 1 Lloyd's Reports 187.

2. On a careful reading of His Honour Judge Thornton's judgment in *Buxton Building Contractors Ltd v Governors of Durand Primary School* [2004] 1 BLR 474, I do not think that this judgment is inconsistent with proposition 1. If, however, Mr Furst is right and if *Buxton* is inconsistent with proposition 1, then I consider that *Buxton* was wrongly decided and I decline to follow it.

3. It is often not practicable for an adjudicator to put to the parties his provisional conclusions for comment. Very often those provisional conclusions will represent some intermediate position, for which neither party was contending. It will only be in an exceptional case such as *Balfour Beatty v the London Borough of Lambeth* that an adjudicator's failure to put his provisional conclusions to the parties will constitute such a serious breach of the rules of natural justice that the Court will decline to enforce his decision.

4. During argument, my attention has been drawn to certain decisions on the duty to give reasons in a planning context. See in particular *Save Britain's Heritage v No 1 Poultry Limited*, [1991] 1 WLR 153 and *South Bucks DC and another v Porter (No 2)* [2004] 1 WLR 1953. In my view, the principles stated in these cases are only of limited relevance to adjudicators' decisions. I reach this conclusion for three reasons:

(a) Adjudicators' decisions do not finally determine the rights of the parties (unless all parties so wish).
(b) If reasons are given and they prove to be erroneous, that does not generally enable the adjudicator's decision to be challenged.
(c) Adjudicators often are not required to give reasons at all.

5. If an adjudicator is requested to give reasons pursuant to paragraph 22 of the Scheme, in my view a brief statement of those reasons will suffice. The reasons should be sufficient to show that the adjudicator has dealt with the issues remitted to him and what his conclusions are on those issues. It will only be in extreme circumstances, such as those described by Lord Justice Clerk in *Gillies Ramsay*, that the court will decline to enforce an otherwise valid adjudicator's decision because of the inadequacy of the reasons given. The complainant would need to show that the reasons were absent or unintelligible and that, as a result, he had suffered substantial prejudice.'

The judge also concluded that paragraph 20(c) of the Scheme gave the adjudicator a freestanding power to award interest.

See also *CIB Properties Ltd v Birse Construction* (2004), summarised at 1.13, in which the court found that the test is whether, taking a common sense approach, the dispute has crystallised. Even after it has crystallised, parties may wish to have further discussions in order to resolve it. Whether or not a dispute has, in fact, crystallised will depend on the facts in each case, including whether or not the parties are in continuing and genuine discussions in order to try to resolve the dispute. The court found as a matter of fact that in the 15 intervening weeks between the notification of the claim and the date of the referral to adjudication, there had been a proper opportunity for Birse to consider the claim and provide a constructive response, which may or may not have led to further discussions. Instead, Birse attempted to manoeuvre tactically so that it could make the claim that the dispute had not crystallised. Both sides had, for a long time before the start of the adjudication, been engaged in tactical manoeuvres. Looking at the history it is impossible to conclude that Birse was ambushed by CIB.

See also *J. W. Hughes Building Contractors Ltd v GB Metalwork Ltd* (2003), summarised at 11.3, in which it was argued that there was no dispute at the time of the purported referral to adjudication. The judge, however, concluded that it was clear that there were outstanding matters relating to GB Metalwork's subcontract claims that were additional to the contract sum and were matters in respect of which it was hoped that J. W. Hughes would then be able to pass the financial responsibility up the line to the employer. The judge concluded that this matter had already been considered by the adjudicator; that there was an ad hoc agreement by the parties to the adjudicator having jurisdiction to deal with jurisdiction; and that therefore there was no need for the judge to elaborate further.

See also *William Verry Ltd v North West London Communal Mikvah* (2004), summarised at 11.4, in which the judge concluded that the nil valuation that had been referred to adjudication was the culmination of a lengthy and contentious process that had started when William Verry had contended that the works were both satisfactorily complete and that practical completion had been achieved, whereas NWLCM's agent had asserted that the works contained significant defects that precluded them from being regarded as complete or as having achieved practical completion. The judge therefore concluded that the adjudication notice referred an existing dispute that had already crystallised to adjudication. The notice was not premature and the adjudicator was validly appointed.

5
The notice of intention
to adjudicate

5.1 DEFINING THE ADJUDICATOR'S JURISDICTION

The adjudicator's jurisdiction is limited to matters raised in the
notice of intention to adjudicate.

Ken Griffin & John Tomlinson (t/a K&D Contractors) v Midas Homes Ltd (2001)

The notice of adjudication referred to the dispute between
the parties but did not clarify what that dispute was. The
defendants argued that there were a number of disputes
between the parties at the time of the notice, and the failure
in the notice to specify which dispute was being referred
was fatal.

The judge concluded that the notice was difficult to interpret
and he was critical of the solicitors who had drafted it.
However, he was clear that at least one dispute between the
parties related to the validity of a notice of determination.
Therefore, on that issue at least, the judge concluded that the
adjudicator had jurisdiction to decide the matter referred.

Total M&E Services Ltd v ABB Technologies Ltd (2002)

The claimant was seeking enforcement of an adjudicator's
decision to the effect that they should be paid the additional
sum of £462,788. In addition, they were seeking to recover
their costs of the adjudication amounting to some £93,000.

ABB defended enforcement proceedings on two principal
bases:

(1) They argued that the referral notice had been made out
    in the name of Total Mechanical And Electrical Services
    Ltd, which was a wholly different company from the

company that ABB were in contact with – namely Total M&E Services Ltd.

(2) They argued that the contract between Total M&E Services Ltd and ABB contained no provision for variation. Therefore all of the additional works being claimed by Total were separate contracts, which could not all be referred in one referral notice.

With regard to point (1), the judge concluded that this is a clear case of description where the claimant and defendant at all stages were aware of the true identities of the contracting parties and no one could be misled. The judge went on to comment that this might not have been so but for the fact that the two companies had nothing to do with one another. Where similarly named companies are part of the same group, precise description of the referring party could be critical.

Total made a claim for their costs incurred in bringing the adjudication and damages for breach of contract. They argued that ABB's failure to pay meant that it was foreseeable that the claimant would seek adjudication and properly incur costs, and thereafter seek to recover them. The judge disagreed and concluded that such costs cannot give rise to a claim as damages for breach.

With regard to point (2), the judge concluded that the adjudicator made his decision on the basis of the dispute arising out of the single written construction contract as varied orally by the parties. The contract as varied is clearly within the provisions of section 107 of the Act, notwithstanding that it is a contract evidenced partly in writing and partly orally. [Note that this decision was produced just before the decision in *RJT Consulting Engineers Ltd v DM Engineering (Northern Ireland) Ltd* (2002), summarised at 1.3.] The adjudicator therefore had jurisdiction to make determinations as to the additional works.

Further, ABB sought set-off and counterclaimed against the adjudicator's decision. This claim was rejected for two reasons. Firstly, the judge concluded that the adjudicator was properly seized of the issues that the claimants were now seeking to reopen. Secondly, the judge concluded that there was inadequate evidence to support the counterclaim in any event.

Finally, ABB sought a stay of execution on the basis of the impecuniosity of the claimant. The judge concluded that the claimant had few fixed assets but that the evidence as to the risk of future non-payment was not based on compelling and uncontradicted evidence. He therefore concluded that there were no special circumstances that rendered it inexpedient to enforce the judgment.

5.2 ONLY ONE DISPUTE AT A TIME

Usually only one dispute at a time can be referred to adjudication, but a single dispute may consist of a number of issues.

Fastrack Contractors Ltd v Morrison Construction Ltd (2000)

Fastrack was a brickwork subcontractor to Morrison as the main contractor. Morrison alleged that Fastrack was behind program and appointed others to expedite part of the works. Fastrack treated this is a repudiating breach and withdrew from site.

Two adjudications ensued in which Fastrack were awarded sums totalling approximately £121,000. Morrison challenged the adjudicator's jurisdiction on the basis that the notice of intention to adjudicate referred to more than one dispute, which, under the Scheme, was not permissible.

The judge concluded that:

- Under the Scheme, if two disputes are to be referred there must be two references. However, a dispute may involve a number of claims.
- A referring party may decide to confine the referred dispute to something less than the totality of the matters in dispute, provided that this does not transform the dispute. A claim can often be made without its quantification having been finalised or even attempted.

- A dispute can only arise once the subject matter of the claim, issue or other matter has been brought to the attention of the opposing party and that party has had an opportunity of considering and admitting, modifying or rejecting the claim of assertion.
- Fastrack's referral notice was wide enough to embrace the whole of the dispute between the parties outstanding after the first adjudication had been completed and accordingly the adjudicator had full jurisdiction.

Barr Ltd v Law Mining Ltd (2002)

This matter arose out of two adjudications: in the first the defenders were ordered to pay the sum of £313,760.84 and in the second the defenders were ordered to pay the sum of £844,742.63.

One issue in each case was whether, if the adjudicator had exceeded his jurisdiction, it was possible to separate the 'good part' from the 'bad part' of a decision, thus allowing the former to be enforced by granting decree for payment. This proposition was agreed by both parties and therefore did not form part of the judgment.

Other issues related to whether more than one dispute was referred in a single notice. The judge accepted that the scheme did not permit more than one dispute to be referred in a single notice but concluded on the facts of this case that the matters referred were in fact several matters relating to a single dispute and did not amount to separate disputes.

There was also an issue as to whether the contract had been rescinded, and if it had what the adjudicator's jurisdiction would be after the rescission. The adjudicator took the view that rescission was a matter for the court alone and therefore made his decision ignoring the alleged rescission. The court decided that the adjudicator would only have had jurisdiction to proceed down this route if he had first decided that there had been no rescission. Having made no such decision, he had no jurisdiction to determine the part of the dispute affected by that issue.

Chamberlain Carpentry & Joinery Ltd v Alfred McAlpine Construction Ltd (2002)

Disputes arose between Chamberlain and McAlpine, which were referred to adjudication. The adjudicator decided that McAlpine should pay Chamberlain the sum of £56,000, however McAlpine refused to pay.

During these proceedings – brought to enforce the decision of the adjudicator – McAlpine argued that the adjudicator's decision was a nullity because Chamberlain had sought to refer several disputes, not just one.

The adjudicator decided that what constitutes a dispute fit to be referred to adjudication as a single dispute is a question of fact. In this case he decided that what Chamberlain referred to adjudication was a dispute as to how much it should be paid by McAlpine.

The judge also concluded that in determining what disputes had been referred to adjudication his enquiries should be limited to the notice of intention to adjudicate and should not extend to the referral notice.

[However, see also *R. Durtnell & Sons Ltd v Kaduna Ltd* (2003), summarised in Chapter 4, in which the judge compared the JCT adjudication scheme in clause 41a of the contract with the Scheme for Construction Contracts and concluded that whilst it was clear that under the Scheme for Construction Contracts only one dispute could be the subject of one notice of adjudication, the same did not apply to the JCT adjudication scheme.]

See also *Costain Ltd v Wescol Steel Ltd* (2003), summarised in Chapter 4; and *AWG Construction Services Ltd v Rockingham Motor Speedway Ltd* (2004), summarised at 9.3.

5.3 TIMING OF ISSUE OF THE NOTICE

The notice of intention to adjudicate can be served at any time but may need to be served before application is made for the appointment of an adjudicator.

Palmac Contracting Ltd v Park Lane Estates Ltd (2005)

Palmac was applying for summary judgment to enforce the decision of the adjudicator concerning an application for payment. Park Lane Estates were resisting enforcement on the following grounds:

(1) There was no dispute at the time of the reference to adjudication, and as such the adjudicator had no jurisdiction to make a valid decision.
(2) The contractual provisions relating to the appointment of the adjudicator were not followed, and this deprives the adjudicator of jurisdiction.
(3) The adjudicator departed from an agreed position between the parties and/or failed to afford the parties the opportunity to comment on this departure. This was a breach of rules of natural justice.

With regard to point (1), Park Lane Estates argued that the application for payment had not been served in accordance with the provisions of the contract. It had been served by e-mail, whereas they contented that it could only be properly served by fax or letter. Park Lane Estates contended that until the application for payment was properly served there could be no dispute in relation to any entitlement pursuant to it.

The judge concluded that this was a point that had been referred to the adjudicator and on which the adjudicator had made a valid decision. Therefore it was not open to the court to go behind the adjudicator's decision and enquire whether the adjudicator had answered the question correctly.

With regard to point (2), Park Lane Estates argued that the contract required notice of adjudication to be given to the defendant before the claimant applied to the Royal Institution of Chartered Surveyors (RICS) for nomination of an adjudicator.

The judge noted that there was nothing in the Act that prevents nomination before notice of adjudication, although adjudication procedures set out in contracts and in the Scheme may do so. In this case the judge concluded that the JCT adjudication procedure did not require notice of adjudication to be served before nomination, and therefore the claimant did not go outside the procedure envisaged by the contract.

With regard to point (3), the judge concluded that the adjudicator had invited submissions, he had incorporated no new material and he had made no investigations of his own. Further, the judge concluded that the adjudicator is permitted at his absolute discretion to take the initiative in ascertaining the facts and the law. That is what the adjudicator did, and did so on the basis of submissions made and information given by the parties. The judge concluded that he was entitled to do so and that there was not a breach of the rules of natural justice.

See also *IDE Contracting Ltd v R G Carter Cambridge Ltd* (2004), summarised in Chapter 6, in which the judge concluded that the Scheme required the notice of adjudication to come first, then the referring party to request the person specified in the contract to act as adjudicator, unless he has already indicated to the parties that he is unwilling or unable to act. The judge further concluded that non-compliance with those provisions deprives the adjudicator of jurisdiction unless the responding party has submitted to the adjudicator's jurisdiction.

See also *Connex South Eastern Ltd v MJ Building Services Group plc* (2005), summarised at 1.10. In this case the Court of Appeal found that a party is entitled to refer the dispute to adjudication at any time, that this means exactly what it says, that therefore there is no time limit and that therefore a late referral was not an abuse of process.

6
Appointing the adjudicator

If the adjudicator is not appointed in accordance with the terms of the applicable scheme then his appointment is invalid and any decision of his will be unenforceable.

Grovedeck Ltd v Capital Demolition Ltd (2000)

Grovedeck referred disputes under two separate oral contracts in a single notice of intention to adjudicate.
The adjudicator decided that payment was due in favour of Grovedeck, and Grovedeck applied for summary judgment to enforce that decision.

In relation to the contracts being oral, the judge concluded that they were therefore not contracts within the scope of the Act and that therefore the adjudicator lacked jurisdiction.

With regard to the notice of adjudication referring to disputes arising under two separate contracts, the judge concluded that if the Act had applied to the contracts, the Scheme would have applied and Grovedeck would have had no right to refer more than one dispute or more than one contract except with the consent of capital.

Therefore, the application for summary judgment was dismissed.

IDE Contracting Ltd v R G Carter Cambridge Ltd (2004)

IDE were applying for summary judgment to enforce the decision of an adjudicator against Carter. Carter defended the application on the basis that the adjudicator had not been properly appointed and therefore lacked jurisdiction.

The contract between the parties provided that a Mr Stephen Pratt would be the adjudicator in any reference between the parties or, in the event of him being unable or unwilling to act, a person nominated by the president or a vice president of the Royal Institute of Chartered Arbitrators (sic).

Mr Stephen Pratt was contacted on behalf of IDE (without notifying Carter) to enquire as to his availability. He replied that he would not be able to accept the appointment as he had work commitments that would be taking him overseas.

It was only in the notice of adjudication that Carter were advised that Mr Stephen Pratt had declined to act as adjudicator.

The judge concluded that the Scheme required the notice of adjudication to come first, then the referring party to request the person specified in the contract to act as adjudicator, unless he has already indicated to the parties that he is unwilling or unable to act. The request must be in writing since it must be accompanied by a copy of the notice of adjudication. What happened here is that no request at all was made pursuant to the Scheme: the procedure was bypassed. The judge concluded that the unwillingness or inability of the specified person to act should be indicated to all parties, otherwise it would be open to the person intending to refer to select a time when the specified adjudicator was or was not available according to his preference.

The judge further concluded that non-compliance with those provisions deprives the adjudicator of jurisdiction unless the responding party has submitted to the adjudicator's jurisdiction.

7
The referral

7.1 THE SCOPE OF THE REFERRAL

The matters raised in the referral must be limited to the scope of the dispute identified in the notice of intention to adjudicate. The adjudicator has no jurisdiction to consider matters not raised in the notice without the implied or express consent of both parties.

John Cothliff Ltd v Allen Build (North West) Ltd (1999)

This was an application for summary judgment pursuant to the decision of an adjudicator operating under the terms of the Scheme.

Cothliff had claimed, and the adjudicator had decided, that the provisions of the Scheme entitled him to award parties' costs. Allen Build refused to comply with this part of the adjudicator's decision.

The judge was reluctant to interfere with the adjudicator's decision, and therefore enforced payment of the parties' costs.

Although it is not clear whether the judge came to his decision because no one submitted to the adjudicator that he had no power to award costs, it has been assumed subsequently that that was the case.

Northern Developments (Cumbria) Ltd v J & J Nichol (2000)

This application followed an adjudication in which the adjudicator decided that J&JN were entitled to payment of approximately £250,000.

Northern Developments brought this application for a declaration that the adjudicator lacked jurisdiction to make some of the decisions that he had made.

One issue raised by Northern Developments was that the adjudicator had failed to consider repudiatory breaches that they had raised. The judge concluded that the adjudicator had no jurisdiction to consider the repudiation claim because it was not mentioned in any notice of intention to withhold payment. The adjudicator did not consider the repudiation claim, though his decision was based on a reason that was wrong in law. Since the adjudicator was quite right in excluding that matter from consideration because he had no jurisdiction to consider the matter, his decision cannot be impeached in that regard even if his reasons were wrong.

Another issue raised by Northern Developments was that the adjudicator was wrong to have awarded parties' costs as part of his decision. The adjudication was governed by the Scheme and the adjudicator had relied on the decision in *John Cothliff* (set out above). The judge concluded that, in general, an adjudicator has no jurisdiction to decide that one party's costs of the adjudication be paid by the other party. However, in the circumstances of this case, the judge concluded that the adjudicator was granted such jurisdiction by implied agreement of the parties.

A J Brenton v Jack Palmer (2001)

Brenton was seeking to enforce the decision of an adjudicator by way of summary judgment.

There was some doubt as to whether the contract was with Mr Jack Palmer or with his company, and this issue had been referred to the adjudicator.

Mr Palmer was defending the application for summary judgment on the basis that the contract was with his company and not with him personally, contrary to the finding of the adjudicator.

The judge concluded that the finding of fact by the adjudicator was one that he was charged to make, and that he had not erred in law in reaching a conclusion that he had jurisdiction, having regard to that finding. Therefore the judge refused to interfere with the decision of the adjudicator.

7.2 LIMITING THE SIZE OF THE REFERRAL

In *Emcor Drake & Scull Ltd v Costain Construction Ltd & Skanska Central Europe AB (t/a Costain Skanska Joint Venture)* (2004), summarised at 1.11, CSJV argued that Emcor had submitted approximately 5,000 pages of information in its referral, to which it was unfair and an abuse of the adjudication process to require CSJV to respond in the second adjudication. The judge decided that the necessity to respond quickly to vast quantities of paperwork is one of the well known hazards of the adjudication process. That cannot of itself be a ground for contending that there has been an abuse of process.

See also *London & Amsterdam Properties Ltd v Waterman Partnership Ltd* (2003), summarised in Chapter 4, in which the contract required the referral notice to be restricted to 20 single-sided A4 pages. In fact the referral exceeded 1,000 pages. Waterman had objected to the size of the referral during the course of the adjudication and the adjudicator had admitted the first 20 pages as the referral and the balance under his jurisdiction to admit further information. The judge concluded that provided the first 20 pages sufficiently identified the dispute that existed the adjudicator was entitled to regard that as a reference compliant with the contract and the Scheme and thereafter to make directions to receive the additional documentation.

7.3 WITHOUT PREJUDICE CORRESPONDENCE

The adjudicator should not be shown without prejudice correspondence between the parties, but disclosure of such correspondence does not necessarily invalidate the process provided that the adjudicator can dismiss it from his mind.

Glencot Development & Design Ltd v Ben Barrett & Son (Contractors) Ltd (2001)

Glencot were appointed by Barrett to supply mild steel wind posts, which Barrett had to provide as part of their brickwork subcontract.

Disputes arose between the parties in relation to the entitlement of Glencot to a claimed additional sum of approximately £350,000, which Glencot referred to adjudication.

During a recess in the adjudication meeting, Glencot and Barrett reached agreement on a valuation of the works but subsequently disputed whether that agreement included a three per cent discount. Parties requested that the adjudicator mediate on this point for them, which the adjudicator agreed to do. From the outset the adjudicator had stated, and the parties had agreed, that the adjudicator would continue with the adjudication if the mediation failed to result in a final agreement.

The adjudicator moved to and fro between the parties, meeting with them and their representatives in the absence of the other party and also meeting the parties together. A figure was agreed in the early evening, but other points (such as time for payment) could not be resolved that day.

During the course of a subsequent meeting, Barrett advised the adjudicator that his position as adjudicator had been compromised by being involved in the mediation or negotiation and that he should withdraw. The adjudicator took counsel's advice and decided not to withdraw.

The adjudicator proceeded to issue his decision, which Glencot sought to enforce by way of summary judgment.

The judge concluded that, for the purposes of the summary judgment application, Barrett had shown that it had real prospects of success in establishing that the adjudicator was no longer impartial as a result of what took place during the course of the mediation. The adjudicator's own appreciation of those events led him to write to the parties asking them to decide whether they wished him to continue. The judge stated that he had reached the conclusion that any fair-minded and informed observer would conclude that the adjudicator's participation in the lengthy discussions during the attempted mediation meant that there was a real possibility of him being biased.

The judge concluded that Barrett had made out a substantial case and that, far from having no real prospect of success, it had, on the present evidence, very good prospects. Moreover, the judge concluded that issues such as these should not be decided on a summary application.

Specialist Ceiling Services Northern Ltd v ZVI Construction (UK) Ltd (2004)

SCS were a subcontractor to ZVI seeking to enforce the decision of an adjudicator by summary judgment.

ZVI were resisting the application for summary judgment on the basis that the adjudicator was shown without prejudice material by SCS's representatives.

The judge concluded, following a review of the response by the adjudicator to the disclosure of without prejudice material, that there was no objective indication of bias or unfairness in this adjudication. The judge concluded that as a result, there was no basis on which to challenge the claim that it should be enforced by judgment.

7.4 WHEN THE RESPONDING PARTY IS IN ADMINISTRATION

Leave of the court is required to refer a matter to adjudication when the responding party is in administration.

Straume (A) (UK) Ltd v Bradlor Developments Ltd (1999)

Bradlor, who were a contractor to Straume, went into administration before the works were complete. Straume attempted to adjudicate against Bradlor, but the judge concluded that as Bradlor were in administration, leave of the court would be required. In this case the court refused leave.

7.5 TIMING OF THE REFERRAL

A contractual procedure must enable a referring party to refer the dispute within seven days of the notice of intention to adjudicate, but may also enable a referring party to defer issue of the referral if it chooses.

In *William Verry Ltd v North West London Communal Mikvah* (2004), summarised at 11.4, the judge concluded that the Act requires that the contractual timescale should have the object of securing the referral of the dispute to the adjudicator within seven days of the adjudication notice. Thus, the statute is setting a minimum requirement for the contract. The contract must allow a referring party, if it chooses, to issue a referral notice within the prescribed seven-day timescale. However, there is nothing in the Act to preclude the contract from being drafted so as to provide additional machinery that enables the adjudicator to extend that timescale and enable the referring party to refer the dispute outside the seven-day period if it chooses to. In other words, the Act requires contractual machinery that enables the referring party to refer the dispute within seven days of the adjudication notice, but it does not prohibit a machinery that additionally enables the referring party to refer the dispute outside that timescale if it elects to take longer in making the reference.

Therefore, in that case and in the light of William Verry's compliance with the adjudicator's procedural direction as to the service of the referral notice, that notice was served within time and the subsequent adjudication and the resultant decision of the adjudicator were not invalidated by the referral notice being served out of time.

8
The response

The adjudicator cannot consider counterclaims unless they are within the scope of the notice of intention to adjudicate – often the referring party will draft the notice of intention to adjudicate deliberately to exclude counterclaims from the scope of the adjudicator's jurisdiction. However, if the counterclaim is raised by way of set-off (that is, as an excuse for not paying the principal sum claimed) then that is a matter that the adjudicator should consider in determining whether or not the principal sum claimed is due and payable.

Farebrother Building Services Ltd v Frogmore Investments Ltd (2001)

This was an application for summary judgment in which Farebrother were seeking to enforce the decision of an adjudicator. The adjudicator had been asked to decide a dispute involving an entitlement to an extension of time and loss and expense.

Frogmore had made a counterclaim on the basis that Farebrother were themselves in critical delay as a result of which Frogmore claimed substantial sums of money in excess of those being claimed by Farebrother.

The adjudicator upheld Farebrother's contention for an extension of time, but stated that he had no jurisdiction to deal with the respondents' counterclaim.

Frogmore did not seek to challenge the adjudicator's award but sought to deduct or set-off the sum that Frogmore put before the adjudicator and that they asserted was not challenged.

The judge concluded that whether or not the adjudicator considered the counterclaim, that is not a matter that goes to jurisdiction. Rather, it is a matter that goes to the conduct of proceedings. The adjudicator may have been wrong, or he may have erred in what he did, but it is an error that is, in principle, within his jurisdiction. He has simply made a decision that is incorrect.

The judge said that it is not right for the court to try and dismantle or reconstruct a decision. Either the adjudicator has jurisdiction or he does not. If he had jurisdiction, this decision is binding even if he was wrong to reach the conclusion he did. The judge therefore concluded that the adjudicator's award ought to be enforced in the sum found by the adjudicator, and that it is not right to set-off the sum the defendant sought to deduct from the award.

William Verry (Glazing Systems) Ltd v Furlong Homes Ltd (2005)

Furlong (the employer) commenced adjudication proceedings against William Verry (the contractor) as to William Verry's entitlement to an extension of time and as to the value of the final account.

William Verry had been making various unparticularised claims in this regard and Furlong no doubt wished to conclude these matters.

William Verry sought to submit particulars relating to their entitlement to an extension of time and loss and expense during the course of the adjudication, to which Furlong objected on the basis that these new particulars were not the basis of the dispute that had been referred to the adjudicator. Notwithstanding these arguments from Furlong, the adjudicator admitted the new information and made his decision accordingly.

William Verry sought to enforce the decision of the adjudicator and Furlong resisted on the basis that the adjudicator had erred in admitting and taking into account the fresh evidence submitted by William Verry during the course of the adjudication.

The judge found in favour of William Verry on the following two grounds:

(1) The judge found that the new particulars submitted on behalf of William Verry did not amount to a new claim, but were simply a fuller explanation of the claim already made.

(2) The judge referred to the adjudication as a 'kitchen sink' final account adjudication in which there was no express limitation or qualification on the range of matters for decision. The judge found further support for this conclusion in the fact that the adjudicator had been asked to decide what extension of time the contractor *is* entitled to. Therefore, the judge found that even if the new particulars submitted by William Verry had amounted to a new claim, they would still have been admissible by the adjudicator to answer the question referred.

It should also be noted that in this case it was the responding party that sought to admit the new information.

9
Subsequent communications with the adjudicator

After the matter has been referred to the adjudicator and the other party has had an opportunity to respond to the material in the referral, the adjudicator will often ask for or admit additional submissions and evidence by the parties. Care is needed in relation to these further submissions to ensure that they do not prevent the adjudicator's decision from being enforced.

9.1   PRIVATE DISCUSSIONS WITH ONE OF THE PARTIES

The adjudicator should not discuss the substantive issues with one party without disclosing the contents of that discussion to the other party and giving the other party an opportunity to present its side of the argument.

Discain Project Services Ltd v Opecprime Developments Ltd (2001)

Discain entered into a contract with Opecprime to design, manufacture and erect steel balconies. Disputes arose, which Discain referred to adjudication. The adjudicator decided that Opecprime should pay to Discain the sum of £65,274.19. Discain were seeking to enforce the decision of the adjudicator, which Opecprime were resisting on the basis that the adjudicator had had a number of telephone conversations with representatives of Discain, which was in breach of the rules of natural justice.

The judge concluded that there was no reason in the law why an adjudicator should not have telephone conversations with individual parties to the adjudication, but that it would make life a great deal easier for him if he declined to do so.

Having considered all of the evidence the judge concluded that the adjudicator did not act in accordance with the rules of natural justice, nor did the adjudicator conduct the proceedings as fairly as the limitations imposed by parliament permit. The limitations imposed by parliament did not require the telephone conversations of which complaint was made. Accordingly, the judge declined to enforce the decision of the adjudicator.

See also *AMEC Capital Projects Ltd v Whitefriars City Estates Ltd* (2004), summarised at 9.2.

9.2 APPARENT BIAS

The adjudicator should conduct himself in a manner so as not to raise any question of apparent bias.

A & S Enterprises Ltd v Kema Holdings Ltd (2004)

The decision of the adjudicator in this case was not enforced by way of summary judgment because it was found that there was a real possibility of bias on the part of the adjudicator.

The key issue before the court related to comments by the adjudicator in his decision in relation to the evidence of a Mr Overend. Mr Overend had not attended a meeting called by the adjudicator or made himself available for interview. In his decision, the adjudicator had said that Mr Overend played a crucial role in the events leading to the dispute. The adjudicator said that Mr Overend's failure to take part in the meeting was very unhelpful and that he therefore viewed the responding party's submissions and the arguments that they had put forward in this light.

The difficulty for the adjudicator was that he had not previously made it clear to either of the parties that he felt it important for him to hear orally from Mr Overend. If the adjudicator had formed this conclusion during the meeting with the parties he ought to have given the responding party an opportunity to make Mr Overend available for oral questioning. Without making clear that he would be influenced to a significant degree by whether he had or had not heard from Mr Overend, when there was no suggestion prior to the meeting with the parties that that was an all-important matter, the adjudicator failed to comply with the requirements of natural justice.

AMEC Capital Projects Ltd v Whitefriars City Estates Ltd (2004), CA

The responding party challenged the decision of the adjudicator on the basis of apparent bias. The test applied by the Court of Appeal was whether a fair-minded and informed observer, having considered all the circumstances that have a bearing on the suggestion that the decision-maker was biased, would conclude that there was a real possibility that he was biased: *Porter v Magill* at paragraph 103.

The adjudicator in this case was initially appointed and made his decision in favour of the referring party. However, that decision was found to be unenforceable because the adjudicator had not been properly appointed. The same adjudicator was subsequently reappointed in a second adjudication concerning the same matters.

The judge at first instance held that there was a real possibility of bias in the present case by reason of the combined effect of the facts that:

(a) on AMEC's case, the issues were the same in the two adjudications;
(b) on the basis of the adjudicator's findings, the issues that he had to decide were the same in both adjudications;
(c) the legal advice obtained in the first adjudication may have been 'carried forward' into the second adjudication and influenced the second decision;
(d) the adjudicator did not give the parties an opportunity to comment on the legal advice obtained on the jurisdiction issue in the second adjudication; and
(e) the adjudicator had a private conversation with the solicitor representing the referring party, which was limited to an explanation of why he was being re-appointed.

The Court of Appeal overturned the decision of the first instance judge on the following grounds:

(a), (b) The mere fact that the tribunal has previously decided the issue is not of itself sufficient to justify a conclusion of apparent bias. Something more is required. The vice that the law must guard against is that the tribunal may approach the rehearing with a closed mind.

(c) This was a new point that had not previously been raised and which was too late to raise now.

(d) Natural justice requires no more than that a party should have an effective opportunity to make representations before a decision is made. In the court's view, Whitefriars had such an opportunity in the present case and took advantage of it. In any event, the common law right to prior notice and an effective opportunity to make representations is to protect parties from the risk of decisions being reached unfairly. But it is only directed at decisions that can affect parties' rights. In this case the legal advice related to the adjudicator's own jurisdiction, which was not binding on the parties.

(e) Conversations between one party and the tribunal in the absence of the other party should be avoided. Communications should ordinarily be in writing with copies to all parties. But the Court of Appeal saw nothing in the circumstances of this conversation, which arose out of an innocuous telephone call to the adjudicator's office, which would lead the fair-minded and informed observer to conclude that what was said would give rise to a real possibility of bias.

See also *Woods Hardwick Ltd v Chiltern Air Conditioning Ltd* (2000), summarised at 9.4, in which the adjudicator had given a witness statement in support of one party's application for summary judgment. In this case the judge concluded that there is no rule to prevent such a course but that if the adjudicator is to retain the confidence of the parties he must scrupulously ensure that his evidence is confined to a neutral, factual account of what transpired in the adjudication. In taking the course that he did in this case, the adjudicator exceeded the requirement of neutrality in two material respects. Firstly, he revealed that he had taken strongly against Chiltern and had decided at an early stage in the adjudication process that Chiltern's case should be dismissed. Secondly, he sought in the witness statement to argue the case of Woods Hardwick and to explain and expand upon the reasons for his decision.

9.3 LIMITING THE SCOPE OF THE ISSUES

Any further submissions should not broaden the scope of the issues beyond those identified in the notice of intention to adjudicate as further amplified in the referral.

AWG Construction Services Ltd v Rockingham Motor Speedway Ltd (2004)

AWG were design and build contractors for Rockingham in relation to a speedway race track. Despite remedial works being undertaken by AWG, problems arose with regard to the dispersal of surface water on the track. Rockingham referred the matter to adjudication and the parties agreed that the dispute should be heard with two others arising out of the same contract.

Rockingham's initial argument was that AWG's choice of subbase under the track had been negligent. However, a few days before the end of the adjudication Rockingham changed its arguments to the effect that the problem was caused by the absence of drainage.

The adjudicator decided in favour of Rockingham in relation to this amended claim and in relation to the other two disputes.

AWG applied to the court for a declaration that the adjudicator's decision was unenforceable on the basis that the adjudicator had no jurisdiction to consider the drainage argument as that was not one of the matters referred to in the notice of intention to adjudicate.

The court held that the adjudicator was not rigidly confined to consider only those matters and arguments specifically referred to in the notice of intention to adjudicate, but that a wide interpretation ought to be given to the word 'dispute'. The test was, what had the parties agreed to refer to adjudication, and, so far as evidence was concerned, on what basis? Each case depended on its own circumstances and the context of the referral. However, where the adjudicator's findings were essentially different to the basis upon which the matter had been referred, that might be relevant to procedural fairness and to the adjudicator's jurisdiction. In the circumstances of the instant case, the basis upon which the adjudicator had found for Rockingham was essentially a different dispute from that originally referred.

In relation to the disputes that were not under challenge, these would be enforced.

McAlpine PPS v Transco (2004)

The adjudicator had decided that Transco should pay McAlpine the sum of £52,119.62 plus VAT as interest for late payment.

McAlpine sought to enforce this decision and applied for summary judgment. Transco resisted the application for summary judgment on the basis that the adjudicator had decided on a matter that was much wider than the dispute referred to in the notice of intention to adjudicate.

The notice of intention to adjudicate claimed interest in the sum of the £69,965.16 because of Transco's failure to certify the amounts due to the referring party by the assessment date and/or the amount that was stated to be due in a certified payment being corrected at a later certificate.

However, the judge concluded that new issues were introduced in the course of the adjudication without the agreement of Transco both by McAlpine and by the adjudicator himself. This evidence was objected to by Transco on the basis that it represented a change in the whole basis on which McAlpine put its claim. The judge was satisfied that the case ultimately put forward by McAlpine represented such a change in the nature of the dispute referred to the adjudicator that Transco had a realistic prospect of arguing successfully either that the adjudicator failed to give a decision that was responsive to the dispute that was referred to him or, put another way, gave a decision on what amounted to a different dispute that had not been referred to him. In either case, the adjudicator acted beyond his jurisdiction.

9.4 GIVING BOTH PARTIES AN EQUAL OPPORTUNITY TO RESPOND

The adjudicator should not use his own investigations or commission expert reports or use his own expertise without first sharing that information with the parties and giving them an opportunity to comment.

Woods Hardwick Ltd v Chiltern Air Conditioning Ltd (2000)

Woods Hardwick were an architect and engineer, Chiltern an air conditioning specialist. Chiltern appointed Woods Hardwick on two projects. Disputes arose in connection with liability for fees, which Woods Hardwick referred to two separate adjudications.

In the first adjudication, Chiltern did not dispute the sum that the adjudicator decided was payable (circa £6,000) but claimed a stay of execution pending the outcome of an action that Chiltern was pursuing against Woods Hardwick in relation to an unrelated third project.

In the second adjudication, but involving the same adjudicator, Chiltern purported to set-off damages that it said that it had incurred by reason of Woods Hardwick's failure to provide an accurate survey drawing, as a result of which the works were set out incorrectly. The total additional fee claim was in the order of £45,000. The adjudicator dismissed Chiltern's abatement and decided that Woods Hardwick should be paid a substantial part of their claim.

In relation to the second adjudication, Chiltern complained that the adjudicator lacked impartiality and had conducted the adjudication in breach of the rules of natural justice in that:

(1) he prevented Chiltern from fairly presenting its case at the meetings;

(2) he took evidence from Woods Hardwick and a third-party that he failed to afford Chiltern an opportunity to comment on; and

(3) he provided a detailed witness statement to Woods Hardwick for use in the enforcement proceedings, which contained partisan views adverse to Chiltern.

With regard to point (1), the judge concluded that Chiltern's representatives had every opportunity to present their case and to answer Woods Hardwick's case.

With regard to point (2), the judge concluded that the adjudicator's reasons for not disclosing this information to Chiltern – namely that he felt that it would not serve any useful purpose to seek Chiltern's view on the additional information as he had witness statements provided by Chiltern and in his view there was no likelihood that these witnesses would have any answer to the additional information he had obtained – were not satisfactory.

The judge concluded that in the context of this adjudication in which so much additional information relied on by the adjudicator had been obtained by the process of telephone interviews with representatives of Woods Hardwick and other subcontractors, there was a clear breach of the statutory requirements.

With regard to point (3) on the provision of a witness statement for these enforcement proceedings in support of one party's case against the other party, the judge concluded that there is no rule to prevent such a course but that if the adjudicator is to retain the confidence of the parties he must scrupulously ensure that his evidence is confined to a neutral, factual account of what transpired in the adjudication. In taking the course that he did, the adjudicator exceeded the requirement of neutrality in two material respects. Firstly, he revealed that he had taken strongly against Chiltern and had decided at an early stage in the adjudication process that Chiltern's case should be dismissed. Secondly, he sought in the witness statement to argue the case of Woods Hardwick and to explain and expand upon the reasons for his decision.

Following the above, the judge dismissed the summary judgment application.

Balfour Beatty Construction Ltd v The Mayor & Burgesses of the London Borough of Lambeth (2002)

Balfour Beatty were seeking to enforce the decision of the adjudicator and applied for summary judgment. Lambeth had deducted approximately £356,000 in liquidated damages and Balfour Beatty disputed their entitlement to do so. This dispute was referred to an adjudicator, who decided that Balfour Beatty were entitled to an extension of time and that therefore Lambeth should pay to Balfour Beatty the sum of approximately £284,000 plus interest. He also decided that Lambeth would be liable for his fees.

Lambeth challenged the adjudicator's decision and resisted enforcement on two principal grounds:

(1) Lambeth alleged that the adjudicator did not act impartially as he did not give Lambeth an opportunity to deal with arguments that had not been advanced by either party even though he relied on them to reach his decision.
(2) It was submitted that the decisions reached were in breach of contract and without jurisdiction in that the adjudicator employed assistants to do work beyond that which the parties had agreed he would employ assistants to do.

The judge found that the adjudicator not only took the initiative in ascertaining the facts but also applied his own knowledge and experience to an appreciation of them and that, in effect, did Balfour Beatty's work for it. The judge reasoned that the adjudicator is entitled to use the powers available to him, but that he may not of his own volition use them to make good fundamental deficiencies in the material presented by one party without first giving the other party a proper opportunity of dealing both with that intention and with the results. The judge concluded that the principles of natural justice as applied to an adjudication may not require a party to be aware of the case that it has to meet in the fullest sense, since adjudication may be inquisitorial or investigative rather than adversarial. However, that does not mean that each party need not be confronted with the main points relevant to the dispute and to the decision.

Further, the judge went on to say that an adjudicator does not act impartially or fairly if he arrives at a decision without having given a party a reasonable opportunity of commenting on the case that it has to meet (whether presented by the other party or thought to be important by the adjudicator) simply because there is not enough time available. An adjudicator, acting impartially and in accordance with the principles of natural justice, ought in such circumstances to inform the parties that a decision could not properly, reasonably and fairly be arrived at within the time and invite the parties to agree further time. If the parties were not able to agree more time, then an adjudicator ought not to make a decision at all and should resign.

The judge concluded that constructing or reconstructing a party's case for that party without confronting the other party with it is such a potentially serious breach of the requirement of either impartiality or fairness that the decision is invalid as it is a not a decision that the adjudicator was authorised to make.

With regard to the use of additional assistants, the judge concluded that Lambeth may have established a breach of contract but they did not establish what the consequences were. The judge said that it was true that what the adjudicator did was not authorised technically, but the judge could not draw the conclusion that the breaches had any material consequence on the decision or that there was any material prejudice to Lambeth or substantial injustice. Had this been the only ground upon which enforcement was resisted, the judge would have considered that it had no realistic prospect of success and that Balfour Beatty's application would have succeeded.

Costain Ltd v Strathclyde Builders Ltd (2003)

Costain had undertaken to construct 45 flats and other works for Strathclyde builders. Disputes arose as to entitlements to an extension of time and liability for liquidated damages, which Costain referred to adjudication. The adjudicator decided that Strathclyde Builders should repay the full amount withheld as liquidated and ascertained damages plus interest.

Costain commenced proceedings to enforce that decision, which were resisted by Strathclyde Builders on the basis that the adjudicator had breached the principles of natural justice and therefore his decision should not be enforced.

Shortly before the adjudicator's decision was due to be published the adjudicator wrote to the parties and asked for a four-day extension of time because he wished to discuss one point in particular with his appointed legal adviser. Costain granted such an extension and the adjudicator subsequently produced his decision. The results of the adjudicator's discussions with his legal adviser were not made known to the parties; nor was either party told of the terms of the discussions that had taken place; nor did either of the parties request to be told the terms of the discussions or to see the results.

Strathclyde Builders argued that the failure by the adjudicator to disclose the substance of that legal advice and to invite comments or submissions thereon prior to arriving at his decision was a breach of the principles of natural justice. They argued that it is possible that the decision might have been influenced by advice that was erroneous, incomplete, irrelevant or otherwise unexceptionable, but which the parties had no opportunity to counter or correct.

The judge concluded that he was of the opinion that the arguments of Strathclyde Builders were sufficient to disclose a breach of the principles of natural justice that had resulted in the possibility of injustice to the parties.

The judge said that it was clear that advice was sought and given, and it was impossible to exclude the possibility that such advice went out with the terms of the parties' submissions. It is only if the possibility of injustice can be excluded that a contravention of the principles of natural justice will be irrelevant. In the judge's opinion, that could not be said of the present case.

Therefore the judge concluded that Strathclyde Builders had a relevant defence to Costain's claim and therefore refused Costain's application for summary judgment.

RSL (South West) Ltd v Stansell Ltd (2003)

Stansell are a building contractor, RSL a steel fabricator. Stansell appointed RSL to undertake structural steel work and staircases in respect of a project in Bristol. Disputes arose between the parties in relation to the entitlement of RSL, including claimed amounts for loss and expense. This dispute was referred to adjudication on behalf of RSL and the adjudicator requested permission to appoint a planning expert.

The parties agreed to the appointment of a planning expert subject to being supplied with copies of the instructions, the responses and any reports.

A report was produced, which was disclosed to the parties and which the parties were given an opportunity to comment on. Having received those comments, the planning expert revised his report and reissued it to the adjudicator, who relied on it in making his decision.

It was contended, on behalf of Stansell, that the decision of the adjudicator was not binding on Stansell because the adjudicator had failed to give the parties an opportunity to comment on the final report of the planning expert before reaching his conclusions. That report had an impact in relation to that part of RSL's claim that related to loss and expense in respect of delay to the completion of the subcontract works.

The judge concluded that it was absolutely essential for an adjudicator, if he is to observe the rules of natural justice, to give the parties to the adjudication the chance to comment on any material, from whatever source, including the knowledge or experience of the adjudicator himself, to which the adjudicator is minded to attribute significance in reaching his decision. The judge held that in the present case it was plain, in the judge's mind, that the adjudicator should not have had any regard to the final report of the planning expert without giving both RSL and Stansell the chance to consider the contents of that report and to comment on it. If the adjudicator needed an extension of the time for his decision to enable him to provide the necessary chance, then he should have explained that to the parties in seeking their consent to an extension. If he had explained that he needed an extension in order to afford the parties an opportunity to comment on the planning expert's final report, and the parties, with knowledge of the significance of the request for an extension, had not agreed to one, the likelihood is that they would be taken to have waived the right to raise an objection that they had not had the opportunity which they had refused.

Having failed to persuade the judge to give summary judgment in respect of the whole of the adjudicator's decision, RSL sought summary judgment in respect of that part of the decision that was not affected by the planning expert's report.

The judge concluded that in those cases where several disputes are properly referred to a single adjudicator in a single notice, it may be possible that a valid objection to the decision in relation to one dispute will not affect the validity and enforceability of the decision in relation to another. However, the judge was not prepared to accept that any decision of an adjudicator to which a valid objection can be taken is severable so as to separate out those parts upon which the objection bites from those parts that are unaffected.

Try Construction Ltd v Eton Town House Group Ltd (2003)

Try were converting a former bank headquarters into a luxury hotel. Eton were the employers. Disputes arose between the parties as to entitlements for extensions of time, loss and expense and liability for liquidated damages, which were referred to adjudication. The adjudicator indicated that he wished to obtain assistance from a programming expert and the parties agreed.

The adjudicator decided in favour of Try, and Try brought these proceedings to enforce that decision by way of summary judgment.

Eton resisted the application for summary judgment on the basis that, among other things, the adjudicator had delegated his decision to the programming expert, and had used his own methodology without bringing that to the attention of the parties.

The judge was referred to the case of *Balfour Beatty v Lambeth* (2002) but distinguished that case on the basis that in *Balfour Beatty* there was no analysis at all put forward by the contractor and the adjudicator without agreement or notice used an entirely independent analysis. In this case the representative of Eton conceded that both parties expected the adjudicator's programming expert to approach his task as a delay expert informed by the collapsed as-built technique insofar as he could on the information available to the adjudicator and elicited by him.

The judge concluded that what the adjudicator did was to consider the evidence, then come to a conclusion based on the evidence before him; the adjudicator's decision was clearly the product of the process that Eton had accepted. Also, that Eton agreed to a process that involved the use of a programming expert using his expertise to consider and analyse the entitlement to an extension of time on an as-built basis. In addition, that Eton had further agreed to the adjudicator, using that analysis, taking into account the concessions made by Eton as to the criticality of the first floor and the defences raised by Eton as to the concurrent and culpable delay.

The judge said that this was a transparent process sensibly and pragmatically agreed by the parties and that, on an analysis of the decision, no matters were considered to be outside the argument developed by the parties.

BAL (1996) Ltd v Taylor Woodrow Construction Ltd (2004)

BAL were a subcontractor to Taylor Woodrow. Disputes in relation to payments arose, which BAL referred to adjudication. The adjudicator decided in BAL's favour and these proceedings were brought by way of an application for summary judgment to enforce that decision.

Taylor Woodrow resisted the application for summary judgment on the basis that the adjudicator had acted in breach of the principles of natural justice.

During the course of the adjudication the adjudicator had advised the parties that he would require legal assistance, but he failed to disclose that advice to the parties before making his decision. This, Taylor Woodrow argued, rendered his decision unenforceable.

The judge concluded that in this case there was no acquiescence to the procedure adopted by the adjudicator, that there was a strong arguable case that there had been a breach of the principles of natural justice and accordingly the application for summary judgment would be refused.

See also *Carillion Construction Ltd v Devonport Royal Dockyard Ltd* (2005), summarised in Chapter 4, in which the court said that it is often not practicable for an adjudicator to put to the parties his provisional conclusions for comment. Very often those provisional conclusions will represent some intermediate position, for which neither party was contending. It will only be in an exceptional case such as *Balfour Beatty v the London Borough of Lambeth* (2002) that an adjudicator's failure to put his provisional conclusions to the parties will constitute such a serious breach of the rules of natural justice that the Court will decline to enforce his decision.

See also *J. W. Hughes Building Contractors Ltd v GB Metalwork Ltd* (2003), summarised at 11.3, in which it was argued that the adjudicator had infringed the rules of natural justice, in particular because J. W. Hughes had not been provided with a certain critical document and the adjudicator had failed to take steps to enable J. W. Hughes to deal with that documentation fully and properly in presenting its own case. The judge found that the adjudicator had satisfied himself that GB Metalwork had done what they were required to do by way of serving documentation on J. W. Hughes's then solicitors. On learning of the missing document the adjudicator had invited J. W. Hughes to raise the matter further with him some six days in advance of the meeting if it was felt that it was necessary to do so. J. W. Hughes did not do so. The adjudicator had got on with the process as the legislation required him to do – that is to say, he dealt with it promptly and fairly and arrived at his decision within the normal tight timescale. Therefore the judge dismissed J. W. Hughes's contentions in relation to their second point.

10
Production of the decision

10.1 JURISDICTION

In *Christiani & Nielsen Ltd v The Lowry Centre Development Company Ltd* (2000) (a summary of which is included at 1.9) it was held that:

> 'It has to be borne in mind when considering whether the parties did reach such an agreement that an adjudicator, faced with a challenge to his own jurisdiction, has a choice as to how to proceed. The adjudicator has three options:
>
> 1. He can ignore the challenge and proceed as if he had jurisdiction, leaving it to the court to determine that question if and when his decision is the subject of enforcement proceedings.
> 2. Alternatively, the adjudicator can investigate the question of his own jurisdiction and can reach his own conclusion as to it. If he was to conclude that he had jurisdiction, he could then proceed to decide the dispute that had been referred to him. That decision on the merits could then be challengeable by the aggrieved party on the grounds that it was made without jurisdiction if the adjudicator's decision on the merits was the subject of enforcement proceedings.
> 3. Having investigated the question, the adjudicator might conclude that he had no jurisdiction. The adjudicator would then decline to act further and the disappointed party could test that conclusion by seeking from the court a speedy trial to determine its right to an adjudication and the validity of the appointment of the adjudicator.'

10.2 **ADDRESSING THE ISSUES REFERRED**

The adjudicator must consider all of the issues referred but must restrict his decision to only those issues referred. Provided that the adjudicator answered the right question, his decision will be enforceable even if he comes to the wrong answer.

Ballast plc v The Burrell Company (Construction Management) Ltd (2001)

The parties had entered into a construction contract pursuant to which a dispute has arisen over entitlement to payment. Ballast were claiming a gross sum of approximately £520,000 more than Burrell had paid.

Of the four issues referred to the adjudicator, the adjudicator decided that two were not valid, one was not applicable and one was not granted.

The judge concluded that it was difficult to understand the adjudicator's decision and to determine on what precise basis he reached his decision that the remedies sought were not valid. So far as he could make sense of what the adjudicator had written, the judge concluded that the adjudicator appeared to have decided that he could not carry out an evaluation, or find any payments due, because the parties had departed from the terms of the preprinted contract in a number of respects. The judge concluded that as a result of that error, the adjudicator misconstrued his powers, and, in consequence, failed to exercise his jurisdiction to determine the dispute. His decision is therefore a nullity.

The judge's decision was upheld on appeal.

Bickerton Construction Ltd v Temple Windows Ltd (2001)

Bickerton were a main contractor, Temple a subcontractor. Bickerton determined the employment of Temple allegedly due to poor quality of installation and then claimed additional costs associated with completing and carrying out remedial works. Temple failed to pay the claims and Bickerton sought to refer the matter to adjudication.

The adjudicator decided how much could be withheld by Bickerton but went on to deduct this sum from the total sum which he had calculated was the total sum due and concluded that there was a net sum due to Bickerton.

Temple asserted that the adjudicator had exceeded his jurisdiction in this latter part of his decision as the parties had not agreed to give the adjudicator jurisdiction to deal with the final account between the parties.

The judge concluded that the adjudicator did not have the right to determine the gross valuation figure from which to deduct payments already made and sums that Bickerton were entitled to withhold. Accordingly, the adjudicator did not have jurisdiction to calculate that a sum of money was actually payable to Bickerton, nor to order that such sum be paid.

Britcon (Scunthorpe) v Lincolnfields Ltd (2001)

Britcon was seeking to enforce the decision of an adjudicator. The adjudication arose out of infrastructure works being carried out by Britcon for Lincolnfields as main contractors. The adjudicator's decision was to the effect that a sum of £260,000 plus VAT and interest should be paid to Britcon.

Lincolnsfields sought to defend the application for summary judgment on the basis that the adjudicator had acted outside his jurisdiction by failing to consider and give effect to material that had been submitted to the adjudicator by Lincolnsfields.

Lincolnsfields had argued during the course of the adjudication that the parties had entered into an oral collateral contract to modify the payment provisions of the contract. During the enforcement proceedings Lincolnsfields argued that the adjudicator had not decided on this issue and therefore his decision was unenforceable.

The judge concluded, as a matter of fact and from a review of the adjudicator's reasons, that he had fairly and squarely dealt with the matters referred to him. For those reasons the judge rejected the contention of Lincolnsfields that the decision that the adjudicator had reached lacked jurisdiction.

Jerome Engineering Ltd v Lloyd Morris Electrical Ltd (2001)

This trial resulted from a failed application for summary judgment of an adjudicator's decision in relation to dispute that had arisen between the parties.

Jerome were subcontractors to Lloyd Morris under the terms of DOM/2. The adjudicator decided that an interim payment of £70,000 should be made to Jerome and that Lloyd Morris should be entirely responsible for payment of his fee.

Lloyd Morris contended that the adjudicator did not have jurisdiction to make the decision that he did because the notice of intention to adjudicate failed to make any request for an interim payment or award.

The adjudicator concluded that whilst the notice of intention to refer does not expressly specify the relief that is sought, neither the defendants nor any officious bystander could conceivably have come to any other conclusion than that the claimants were referring to adjudication because they wanted payment of that which, at least on an interim basis, was due to them. Therefore, the judge concluded that for the purposes of the contract, whilst not expressly setting out the relief sought, the notice must be interpreted as being a notice of intention to refer to adjudication for the purposes of recovering money pursuant to an interim award.

LPL Electrical Services Ltd v Kershaw Mechanical Services (2001)

LPL were seeking to enforce the decision of the adjudicator by applying for summary judgment. Kershaw were seeking to resist the application on the basis that the adjudicator did not have jurisdiction to make the decision that he did.

The argument in relation to jurisdiction arose out of a technical interpretation of the contractual provision relating to interim payments. The adjudicator was asked to decide how much was due pursuant to interim application number eight, and arrived at a sum of approximately £70,000 by valuing the works and deducting the amount already paid. Kershaws argued that this was not a decision that was within the scope of the adjudicator's jurisdiction. They argued that the contract required the adjudicator to value the amount due pursuant to an interim application by deducting the sum that was due under the previous application and not the sum that was paid. Applying this methodology, Kershaws concluded that the amount payable pursuant to interim application number eight was no more than £172.

The judge concluded that it was clear that the claimant was asking for payment of the sum of £70,000 and that therefore it was within the jurisdiction of the adjudicator to decide that that sum was due. Whether or not the adjudicator's interpretation of the contract was correct, the decision that he made was within his jurisdiction. Judgment was therefore given for LPL.

Mecright Ltd v T A Morris Developments Ltd (2001)

Mecright were seeking to enforce the decision of an adjudicator that they should be paid a sum of approximately £36,000 by Morris together with interest as damages for Morris's repudiation of the subcontract.

Morris were resisting the application for summary judgment on the basis that the adjudicator exceeded his jurisdiction in deciding that Mecright were entitled to be paid damages.

Morris had terminated the subcontract of Mecright, asserting that Mecright had failed to proceed with their works in a reasonable and workmanlike manner.

Mecright refuted Morris's entitlement to terminate their subcontract, as a result of which Morris referred the dispute to adjudication. Morris claimed in the notice of intention to adjudicate a declaration from the adjudicator that the sub-contract was cancelled in accordance with the subcontract, and secondly, recovery of damages from the respondent arising out of the cancelled subcontract.

Mecright's response in the adjudication sought, amongst other things, payment to Mecright of approximately £58,000.

The adjudicator decided that Morris in fact repudiated the subcontract by instructing Mecright to cease works, and that as a result Morris should pay Mecright the sum of approximately £26,000 plus VAT as a consequence.

The judge concluded that in the present case the essence of the dispute described in the notice was, first, whether in the circumstances Morris had been entitled to determine its contract with Mecright, and, if so, what sum Morris was entitled to be paid by Mecright in consequence of the determination.

The judge accepted the argument that how much Mecright was entitled to be paid in respect of the execution of the subcontract works or as a result of a wrongful determination of the contract by Morris was not, on a proper construction of the notice, covered by the disputes referred. The judge therefore found in favour of Morris, declining to enforce the decision of the adjudicator on the ground that the adjudicator had no jurisdiction to decide what sum was due to Mecright in respect of the execution of the subcontract works.

S. L. Timber Systems Ltd v Carillion Construction Ltd (2001)

This matter arose out of the enforcement of three adjudicators' decisions in relation to three claims on three contracts. Each of the claims related to the supply and erection of structural timber kits by S. L. Timber to Carillion.

Carillion sought to resist the enforcement of the adjudicators' decisions on two grounds:

(1) They argued that the adjudicator had misunderstood the effect of sections 110 and 111 of the Act, that he fell into error, which led him to mistake the true scope of his jurisdiction.
(2) They sought to resist enforcement of the adjudicator's decision on the basis of the financial standing of S. L. Timber.

In relation to point (1), the adjudicator had concluded that because Carillion had not served notices pursuant to sections 110 and 111 of the Act that S. L. Timber were therefore entitled to payment of the sum applied for.

The judge concluded that the adjudicator fell into error by interpreting sections 110 and 111 of the Act as he had. The judge held that the adjudicator ought properly to have held that Carillion's failure to give a section 110 notice was irrelevant to the question of the scope for disputes about S. L. Timber's claims. However, the judge came to the conclusion that the adjudicator's error did not take him out of the proper scope of his jurisdiction. The adjudicator was asked to determine whether Carillion had failed to give a timeous notice of intention to withhold payment. He answered that question in the affirmative. The question that then arose for his consideration was whether, in that event, Carillion were obliged to pay the sums claimed. He addressed that question, and answered it too in the affirmative. His reason for giving that answer to that part of the issue before him lay in the view he took of the effect of section 111, a view that the judge held to be erroneous. However, that was an erroneous answer that he gave after asking himself the right question, in the sense of the question referred to him for decision. The judge was therefore of the opinion that the adjudicator made an intra vires error rather than one that rendered his decision ultra vires. The adjudicator's decision was wrong, but not in such a way as to be invalid.

With regard to the solvency issue, the judge was reluctant to apply the reasoning in English decisions and concluded that Carillion's assertions to the effect that S. L. Timber were insolvent did not constitute a relevant defence.

Martin Girt v Page Bentley (2002)

Martin Girt was seeking to enforce the decision of an adjudicator by way of summary judgment that he be paid the sum of approximately £18,000.

The adjudicator had decided that Martin Girt was entitled to the sum of approximately £59,000 but had reduced this to a sum of approximately £18,000 on the basis of Martin

Girt's Construction Industry Scheme (CIS) tax registration certificate. In fact this reduction was incorrect and no such deduction should have been made.

The reduction made by the adjudicator was not a matter on which the parties had made representations. In the words of Page Bentley, the adjudicator went off on a frolic of his own. He was adjudicating upon matters clearly outside his jurisdiction, which, they argued, taints and fatally affects his award.

The judge concluded that if anybody had cause to complain that the adjudicator went off on a frolic of his own, albeit with the best of intentions, it is Martin Girt because he had no opportunity to address the adjudicator as to the significance of the tax position and to produce a researched argument in relation to that matter.

Any prejudice resulting from an arguable breach of natural justice was visited on the claimant. There was no arguable prejudice to the defendant.

In the circumstances the application for summary judgment succeeded.

Shimizu Europe Ltd v Automajor Ltd (2002)

Shimizu had agreed to undertake works for Automajor involving the design and construction of a three-storey building. Disputes arose as to the entitlement of Shimizu to additional payment, which Shimizu referred to adjudication. The adjudicator decided that Shimizu were entitled to an additional sum of £321,300.99. Automajor failed to pay, so Shimizu commenced proceedings to enforce that decision and applied for summary judgment.

From the reasons given by the adjudicator it was apparent that he had included in his decision an amount of approximately £162,000 in respect of alleged variations, which he had held were not variations. Further, he had made no allowance for a without prejudice payment on account in connection with the alleged variations of £50,000.

Solicitors acting on behalf of Automajor had, immediately after receipt of the adjudicator's decision, written to the adjudicator asking him to correct his decision under the slip rule. However, the adjudicator did not accept that there had been any slip or error in his decision and therefore refused to do so.

Automajor sought to argue that the mistakes made by the adjudicator went to his jurisdiction and vitiated his determination. The judge held that this line of argument was not correct and that the adjudicator's mistakes did not go to his jurisdiction. However, the judge was satisfied that the reason that the adjudicator had awarded sums in respect of alleged variations, which he had held were not variations, was that the adjudicator had formed the belief that the parties had extended his jurisdiction so as to enable him to take account of Shimizu's claim in relation to these variations, which would not otherwise have been proper.

As far as this line of argument was concerned, the judge concluded that the adjudicator had been asked to decide what sum was payable by Automajor to Shimizu, and he had answered that question. If the adjudicator had made a mistake as to the evaluation of what sum, if any, should be paid, that was not a mistake as to what he was being asked to decide. He asked himself the correct question and he answered that question. The proper mechanism for correcting an error, if there is one, is in the course of a final accounts negotiation or in arbitration proceedings; it is not to challenge the award on jurisdictional grounds.

The judge therefore gave judgment for Shimizu.

The judge then went on to consider Shimizu's alternative argument, which was that Automajor had made a part payment against the adjudicator's decision and in so doing had waived their rights to object to it. The judge concluded, in this respect, that it cannot be right that it is open to a party to an adjudication simultaneously to approbate and to reprobate a decision of the adjudicator. Assuming that good grounds exist in which a decision may be subject to objection, either the whole of the relevant decision must be accepted or the whole of it must be contested.

Joinery Plus Ltd (in administration) v Laing Ltd (2003)

Laing entered into two separate subcontracts with Joinery Plus to carry out works. Disputes concerning each subcontract had been referred to the same adjudicator. He had made awards in favour of Joinery Plus in each case and they had been paid.

However, Joinery Plus then sought a declaration from the court as to whether the decision in the second adjudication was valid, claiming that the adjudicator had based his decision on the wrong subcontract conditions. The court held that the adjudicator had resorted to the wrong contract conditions when considering significant parts of the question referred to him. These were fundamental errors, not capable of correction under his implied power to correct accidental slips, rather than mere errors of law within his jurisdiction. The decision was thus a nullity and made without jurisdiction. When an adjudicator gives reasons, they may be used to construe and understand his decision. In this case, the adjudicator's reasons indicated that his errors were so substantial that they affected the validity of the decision. Joinery Plus's receipt of Laing's cheque did not mean that it had accepted or approbated the adjudicator's decision, as it had made clear that it was challenging the decision and that it was accepting the cheque only generally, on account of Laing's obligations under the subcontract. Joinery Plus did not have to repay the money to Laing, as Joinery Plus had a set-off and an equitable cross-claim in the same amount. Joinery Plus could refer the same dispute to another adjudicator. Finally, paragraph 9(2) of the Scheme for Construction Contracts (which requires an adjudicator to resign if the dispute is the same as one that was previously referred and a decision was made) did not apply, as the decision was a nullity.

10.3 TIME FOR PRODUCTION OF THE DECISION

The adjudicator must provide his decision within the required timescale. Minor delays may be excused, as may delay to which the parties have given their actual or tacit consent.

St Andrews Bay Development Ltd v HBG Management Ltd (2003)

The adjudicator's decision was due to be released on 5 March 2003. As there had been no decision published by 5 p.m. on that day, enquiry was made by HBG and they were advised that the adjudicator did not intend to release her decision until her fee had been paid. However, she had not had time to issue her invoice.

At 9 p.m. that evening the adjudicator issued her invoice for her fee and by fax dated 6 March HBG indicated its intention to pay the whole fee in order to secure the release of her decision.

The adjudicator then released her decision by fax on 7 March 2003 with reasons communicated to the parties on 10 March 2003. At no time did the adjudicator seek an extension of the time required to produce a decision beyond 5 March 2003.

In these proceedings St Andrews Bay sought a declaration challenging the adjudicator's decision on the basis that she had no power to reach her decision after 5 March 2003.

The judge concluded that the adjudicator was required to reach a decision by 5 March 2003 and had failed to do so. Although she had completed her consideration of the matter by that date, she made no effort to communicate her decision to the parties or to intimate the fact that she had arrived at the decision at that time.

Neither can it be said that the adjudicator was entitled to delay communication or intimation of the decision until her fees were paid, unless she comes to a separate agreement with the parties to that extent.

However, the judge concluded that while the failure of an adjudicator to produce a decision within the time limits is undoubtedly a serious matter, he did not think that it was of sufficient significance to render the decision a nullity. The production of a decision two days outside the time limit provided is not such a fundamental error or impropriety that it would vitiate the entire decision. Such a failure is a technical matter, and it is of significance in the present case that no challenge is offered to the merits of the adjudicator's decision.

Therefore the judge refused to declare the decision invalid.

Simons Construction Ltd v Aardvark Developments Ltd (2003)

The adjudicator published a draft decision at the end of the 28-day period and produced his final decision in substantially the same format seven days later. The parties had not agreed to any extension of time. The adjudicator found substantially in favour of Aardvark, and this application was bought by Simons for a declaration that the adjudicator's decision was produced out of time and was therefore invalid.

The judge concluded that the draft decision was not a decision for the purposes of adjudication, as it was not signed or dated and it was marked as 'for the parties' comment'.

Following an interpretation of the JCT adjudication agreement, the judge concluded that until the giving of a fresh referral notice, the original adjudicator retains jurisdiction to determine the dispute. Therefore, the decision of an adjudicator for the purposes of the JCT adjudication agreement is binding upon the parties to the relevant dispute whenever given, provided only that the adjudication agreement, if any, has not been terminated for failure to produce a decision within the relevant timescale before the decision is made.

Therefore, the judge held that the final decision signed by the adjudicator was a decision on the dispute referred to him and was binding upon the parties.

Barnes & Elliot Ltd v Taylor Woodrow Holdings Ltd (2004)

The adjudicator had decided that Barnes & Elliott should be paid approximately £655,000 plus interest in relation to the dispute that had been referred to him.

The adjudicator had reached his decision on the basis that the liquidated damages stated in the contract were not a genuine pre-estimate of the loss.

Taylor Woodrow were not happy with this decision but the only basis on which they could develop an argument that it should not be enforced was that the adjudicator's decision had been released two days too late. It was admitted that this was an argument based on a technicality and that no serious prejudice had been done to Taylor Woodrow as a result of this delay.

The judge concluded that whilst time remains very important, an error that results in a day, or possibly two days, seems to be excusable. The judge concluded that such an error was within the tolerance and commercial practice that one must afford to the Act and to the contract. Whilst an adjudicator is not authorised to make mistakes, a decision arrived at in time and which is in principle authorised and valid does not become unauthorised and invalid because an error by the adjudicator in dispatching the decision means that it has not reached the parties within the time limit. However, the judge emphasised that the tolerance does not extend to any longer period (unless perhaps the parties had agreed to a very long duration), nor does it entitle an adjudicator not to complete the decision within the time allowed. If the adjudicator cannot arrive at a decision on all aspects of the dispute within the period required then, before time runs out, further time must be obtained as provided by the contract or otherwise by the parties' agreement.

The judge concluded, therefore, that the decision was enforceable.

Ritchie Brothers (PWC) Ltd v David Philp (Commercials) Ltd (2005)

The expiry of the 28 days for the adjudicator's decision in this case was 16 October 2003. On 21 October 2003 the responding party wrote to the adjudicator challenging his jurisdiction. The adjudicator's response was to request an extension of time to 23 October 2003, to which the referring party agreed. On 23 October 2003 the adjudicator indicated that his decision was ready and requested payment of his fee. Following payment of the adjudicator's fee by the referring party, the adjudicator's decision was released to the parties on 27 October 2003.

The judge made the following decisions:

(1) Under the Scheme, the commencement of the 28-day period was the date on which the referral notice is dated and not the date on which it was received by the adjudicator.

(2) The adjudicator's decision was made on 23 October 2003 and not on 27 October 2003 when it was released to the parties. The judge was referred to, but preferred not to follow, the decision in *St Andrews Bay Development Ltd v HBG Management Ltd* (2003).

(3) The expiry of the 28-day period prior to the referring party's consent to an extension of time did not, under the Scheme, render the adjudicator functus officio (i.e., no longer able to act having discharged all of his functions) but this did entitle either party to serve a fresh referral notice and a new adjudicator could be appointed. That was not done, so the adjudicator's decision was enforced.

On appeal, on point (3) only, the Inner House decided by majority of two-to-three that under the Scheme the adjudicator was required to reach his decision within 28 days of the date of the referral. Unless he received an extension of time prior to the expiry of this period any decision issued later than 28 days would be outside of the adjudicator's jurisdiction and therefore unenforceable.

10.4 THE SLIP RULE

The adjudicator can correct obvious or minor errors in his report provided that he does so very soon after producing it.

Bloor Construction (UK) Ltd v Bowmer & Kirkland (London) Ltd (2000)

Bowmer & Kirkland as main contractors entered into a subcontract with Bloor. Disputes arose, which were referred to adjudication. On the last day of the adjudication period the adjudicator issued his decision to the effect that Bowmer & Kirkland should pay to Bloor the sum of approximately £122,000 within 14 days of the decision.

On the same day, Bowmer & Kirkland notified the adjudicator that he had omitted to take into account various sums paid by them. The adjudicator admitted this mistake and corrected his decision, which was issued later that same evening. The result of the amended decision was that Bloor had been slightly overpaid for the work that they had done, but that as they were continuing to work, this overpayment should not be paid back to Bowmer and Kirkland.

Bloor sought to enforce the first decision of the adjudicator, arguing that once the adjudicator had made his decision it was not open to him to revisit and amend it.

The judge concluded that it was clear that the error in this case falls into the category of a slip. The adjudicator was giving effect to his first thoughts and intentions in his amended ruling. In the absence of any specific agreements to the contrary, the judge held that a term can and should be implied into the contract referring the dispute to adjudication that the adjudicator may, on his own initiative or on the application of a party, correct an error arising from an accidental error or omission.

See also *CIB Properties Ltd v Birse Construction* (2004), summarised at 1.13, in which the court concluded that in relation to a slip or alleged slip there are two questions: (a) Is the adjudicator prepared to acknowledge that he has made a mistake and correct it? (b) Is the mistake a genuine slip, which failed to give effect to his first thoughts? If the answer to both questions is 'Yes', then (subject to the important question of the time within which the correction is made and questions of prejudice) the court can, if the justice of the case so requires, give effect to the amendment to rectify the slip. If the adjudicator is not prepared to make a correction promptly, that is an end of the matter.

10.5 **INTEREST**

In *Carillion Construction Ltd v Devonport Royal Dockyard Ltd* (2002), summarised in Chapter 4, the judge concluded that paragraph 20(c) of the Scheme gave the adjudicator a freestanding power to award interest.

The adjudicator may also award interest pursuant to the *Late Payment of Commercial Debts (Interest) Act* 1998.

11
Enforcement or avoidance of the decision

11.1 APPROBATION AND REPROBATION

If the decision is enforceable, then the whole decision is enforceable. It is not possible to cherry-pick enforceable parts of the decision from unenforceable parts.

KNS Industrial Services (Birmingham) Ltd v Sindall Ltd (2000)

KNS were mechanical and electrical subcontractors to Sindall. KNS considered that they had been underpaid, and therefore served notice of intention to suspend performance of their works and subsequently withdrew from site. Sindall responded by terminating the employment of KNS. KNS referred the matter to adjudication, claiming a proper valuation of their work and asserting that no timely and valid notice of intention to withhold payment had been served.

The adjudicator found that KNS's works had been undervalued by Sindall but that the final date for payment in respect of that valuation had not passed at the time that KNS served their notice of adjudication. The adjudicator found that the final date for payment was 10 March 2000, the notice having been served on 9 March – after the last date for the issue of a withholding notice. The adjudicator then allowed deduction of the sums claimed by Sindall.

Sindall paid the balance that the adjudicator found to be due – £4,844.94.

KNS were dissatisfied with this outcome and sought to enforce that part of the adjudicator's decision that found their works to be undervalued whilst arguing that the adjudicator had exceeded his jurisdiction by taking into account the sums that Sindall sought to withhold. Both parties made separate applications for summary judgment.

The judge concluded that whilst there may be instances where an adjudicator's jurisdiction is in question and the decision can be severed so that the authorised can be saved and the unauthorised set aside, this was not such a case. The judge said that a party cannot pick amongst the reasons so as to characterise parts as unjustified and therefore made without jurisdiction.

The judge therefore gave summary judgment for Sindall against KNS and refused summary judgment for KNS against Sindall.

See also *Shimizu Europe Ltd v Automajor Ltd* (2002), summarised at 10.2, in which the judge considered Shimizu's alternative argument, which was that Automajor had made a part payment against the adjudicator's decision and in so doing had waived their rights to object to it. The judge concluded, in this respect, that it cannot be right that it is open to a party to an adjudication simultaneously to approbate and to reprobate a decision of the adjudicator. Assuming that good grounds exist in which a decision may be subject to objection, either the whole of the relevant decision must be accepted or the whole of it must be contested.

However, see also *R. Durtnell & Sons Ltd v Kaduna Ltd* (2003), summarised in Chapter 4, in which the court held that the principle of approbation and reprobation was a principle that did apply to adjudication. However, in that case Durtnell had referred several disputes and it was open to them without falling foul of that principle to accept the adjudicator's decision in relation to some of those disputes whilst challenging it in relation to others.

See also *RSL (South West) Ltd v Stansell Ltd* (2003), summarised at 9.4, in which the judge concluded that in those cases where several disputes are properly referred to a single adjudicator in a single notice, it may be possible that a valid objection to the decision in relation to one dispute will not affect the validity and enforceability of the decision in relation to another. However, the judge was not prepared to accept that any decision of an adjudicator to which a valid objection can be taken is severable so as to separate out those parts upon which the objection bites from those parts that are unaffected.

11.2 ERRORS IN THE DECISION

The decision of an adjudicator will be enforced even if it is demonstrably wrong provided that the adjudicator has not exceeded his jurisdiction.

Bouygues UK Ltd v Dahl-Jensen UK Ltd (1999)

This was an application for summary judgment to enforce the decision of an adjudicator. Dahl-Jensen resisted the application on the basis that the adjudicator had made an error on the face of his decision.

The dispute related to the amount of money owing between the parties. The adjudicator valued the works and then deducted the value of the previous valuation. Unfortunately, the adjudicator made a mistake by deducting the previous valuation before deduction of retention whereas he had deducted retention from the total value of the works that he had calculated. The result was that he found that a net sum of approximately £208,000 was due in favour of Dahl-Jensen, whereas if the error were corrected he should have found that a net sum of approximately £141,000 was due in favour of Bouygues.

The judge concluded that the adjudicator simply made a mistake in calculating the overpayment. There can be no doubt that what the adjudicator was doing in his counterclaim analysis was calculating the amount of the overpayment. That was an issue that had been referred to him. He was doing precisely what he had been asked to do, and was answering the right question, but he was doing so in the wrong way.

133

In subsequent correspondence the adjudicator said that he did not make a clerical mistake or slip and therefore refused to apply the slip rule.

The judge concluded that the purpose of adjudication is to provide a speedy mechanism for settling disputes in construction contracts on a provisional interim basis, and requiring the decisions of adjudicator to be enforced pending final determination of disputes by arbitration, litigation or agreement, whether those decisions are wrong in point of law or fact. It is inherent in the scheme that injustices will occur, because from time to time, adjudicators will make mistakes. Sometimes those mistakes will be glaringly obvious and disastrous in their consequences for the losing party. The victims of mistakes will usually be able to recoup their losses by subsequent arbitration or litigation, and possibly even by a subsequent adjudication. Sometimes they will not be able to do so, where, for example, there is intervening insolvency, either of the victim or of the fortunate beneficiary of the mistake.

The judge therefore gave Dahl-Jensen summary judgment in respect of the adjudicator's decision.

C & B Scene Concept Design Ltd v Isobars Ltd (2002), CA

This was a decision of the Court of Appeal following the Technology and Construction Court's decision not to enforce the decision of an adjudicator by way of summary judgment.

C & B were the design and build contractors for Isobars in relation to the design, construction and fitting out of a café-bar. C & B were appointed under the JCT With Contractor's Design Standard Form of Contract with bespoke amendments. In particular, the payment provisions had been amended. By erroneously applying the contract in its unamended form the adjudicator concluded that C & B were entitled to be paid the full amount for which they had applied because Isobars had failed to issue a counter notice in time.

The Court of Appeal concluded that the enforcement of an adjudicator's decision by summary judgment should not be prevented by arguments that the adjudicator had made errors of law in reaching his decision, unless the adjudicator had purported to decide matters that were not referred to him. In the present case, there was an entire agreement as to the scope of the dispute, and the adjudicator's decision, although he may have made errors of law as to the relevant contractual provisions, is still binding and enforceable until the matter is corrected in the final determination.

For these reasons the appeal was allowed and the adjudicator's decision was enforced.

See also *Joinery Plus Ltd (in administration) v Laing Ltd* (2003), summarised at 10.2, in which the court held that the errors of the adjudicator were so fundamental as to go to his jurisdiction. In that case it was held that the adjudicator's decision was a nullity.

11.3 INSOLVENCY OF THE RECEIVING PARTY

If the receiving party is insolvent, the court may refuse to enforce the decision of the adjudicator or may require that sums be paid into a stakeholder account.

Harwood Construction Ltd v Lantrode Ltd (2000)

Lantrode sought to resist the enforcement of an adjudicator's decision on three grounds: firstly, on the basis that there was on-going litigation between the parties; secondly, it was claimed that Lantrode had a right to set off against the sum that the adjudicator decided was due; and thirdly, Lantrode claimed that Harwood was or maybe insolvent.

With regard to the first ground, the judge dismissed this on the basis that adjudication is intended to determine the dispute on an interim and temporary basis pending resolution in other proceedings by litigation or arbitration.

With regard to the second ground, the judge followed the course taken in previous decisions by refusing to allow set-off.

With regard to the third ground, a winding-up petition had been presented and a hearing was scheduled for two weeks after the hearing for the summary judgment application. The judge concluded that the evidence before him was insufficient to enable him to be confident of whether the winding-up petition would succeed or fail. In the circumstances, the judge granted the summary judgment but stayed execution until after the hearing of the petition to wind-up Harwood.

Rainford House Ltd (in administrative receivership) v Cadogan Ltd (2001)

Rainford were seeking to enforce the decision of an adjudicator to the effect that Cadogan should pay a sum of £77,350.75.

Rainford were in administrative receivership at the time of the application for summary judgment, which Cadogan relied upon in its claim for resisting the application.

The judge concluded that the evidence before him raised a strong prima facie case that Rainford were insolvent. That evidence had not been contradicted or explained. He therefore drew the inference that the present financial position of Rainford, as revealed by the evidence put before him, would not change, so he concluded that Rainford would be unable to repay the amount that the adjudicator decided was due.

The judge concluded that the appropriate course in the present case was to give summary judgment, but with a stay of execution pending the trial of the counterclaim subject to Rainford being given leave to apply in relation to the lifting of the stay to cover the possibility that Rainford may be able and willing to provide security for the repayment of an amount up to the sum that would otherwise be due.

Baldwins Industrial Service plc v Barr Ltd (2002)

Baldwins hired to Barr a 50-tonne crane, together with the driver, to be used by Barr at a building site. An incident occurred in which the crane was damaged. Baldwins sought from Barr the cost of repairs and lost hire charges, which Barr refused to pay. Baldwins referred the dispute to adjudication. The adjudicator decided that Barr were liable for approximately £185,000.

Shortly after the adjudicator published his decision, joint administrative receivers were appointed to Baldwins who subsequently sought to enforce the adjudicator's decision.

Barr raised two arguments in their attempts to resist summary judgment. Firstly, they argued that the hire of the crane was not a 'construction contract' within the terms of the Act. Secondly, they argued that there should be a stay of execution because of the appointment of administrative receivers to Baldwins.

With regard to the first point, the judge concluded that the contract was not one of mere delivery of plant to site but was for the supply of plant and labour. The contract was therefore a 'construction contract' within the meaning of the Act, and accordingly the adjudicator had jurisdiction.

With regard to the second point, the court agreed to stay execution of the principal sum awarded for a period of one month, subject to the following conditions:

(1) That Barr pay the principal sum into court within seven days.
(2) That Barr commence proceedings within one month from the date of judgment, failing which the money would be paid out to Baldwins.

J W Hughes Building Contractors Ltd v GB Metalwork Ltd (2003)

This matter arose out of a subcontract for the fabrication and erection of steelwork. GB Metalwork made this application for summary judgment of an adjudicator's decision by way of a counterclaim to court proceedings commenced by J. W. Hughes.

J. W. Hughes resisted the application for summary judgment on three grounds:

(1) They argued that there was no dispute at the time of the purported referral to adjudication.

(2) They argued that the adjudicator infringed the rules of natural justice, in particular because they had not been provided with a certain critical document and the adjudicator had failed to take steps to enable J. W. Hughes to deal with that documentation fully and properly in presenting its own case.

(3) It was argued that GB Metalwork were on the brink of insolvency and would not be able to pay the money back in subsequent proceedings.

With regard to point (1), the judge concluded that it was clear that there were outstanding matters relating to GB Metalwork's subcontract claims that were additional to the contract sum and were matters in respect of which it was hoped that J. W. Hughes would then be able to pass the financial responsibility up the line to the employer. The judge concluded that this matter had already been considered by the adjudicator; that there was an ad hoc agreement by the parties to the adjudicator having jurisdiction to deal with jurisdiction; and that therefore there was no need for the judge to elaborate further.

With regard to point (2), J. W. Hughes had changed their solicitors part-way through the adjudication and did not have copies of the documentation accompanying the referral, which had been mislaid by the original solicitors. The importance of this omission did not fully come to light until both parties attended a meeting with the adjudicator.

The missing documentation had been highlighted to the adjudicator at an earlier stage; the adjudicator had invited J. W. Hughes to raise the matter further with him some six days prior to the meeting. However no further representations were made.

The adjudicator had satisfied himself that GB Metalwork had done what they were required to do by way of serving documentation on J. W. Hughes's then solicitors. He had invited J. W Hughes to raise the matter further with him some six days in advance of the meeting if it was felt that it was necessary to do so. J. W. Hughes did not do so. The adjudicator had got on with the process as the legislation required him to do – that is to say, he dealt with it promptly and fairly and arrived at his decision within the normal tight timescale. Therefore the judge dismissed J. W. Hughes's contentions in relation to their second point.

With regard to point (3), the judge was faced, on the one hand, with company accounts lodged at Companies House and credit ratings given by an independent credit trading organisation, and on the other hand by letters from GB Metalwork's accountants and bank stating that the financial position of the company was expected to improve and that it was anticipated that the overdraft facility would be extended.

The judge therefore formed the view that this was not a case in which it can be said that there was a high risk of a present inability to pay the money in the event that GB Metalwork were ordered, as the result of the resolution of underlying dispute, to return any or all of the money that the adjudicator's decision had made available to them as a result of the adjudication process.

Wimbledon Construction Company 2000 Ltd v Derek Vago (2005)

In this case the judge reviewed the previous authorities and summarised the applicable principles as follows:

'a) Adjudication (whether pursuant to the 1996 Act or the consequential amendments to the standard forms of building and engineering contracts) is designed to be a quick and inexpensive method of arriving at a temporary result in a construction dispute.

b) In consequence, adjudicators' decisions are intended to be enforced summarily and the claimant (being the successful party in the adjudication) should not generally be kept out of its money.

c) In an application to stay the execution of summary judgment arising out of an Adjudicator's decision, the Court must exercise its discretion under [RSC] Order 47 with considerations a) and b) firmly in mind (see *AWG*).

d) The probable inability of the claimant to repay the judgment sum (awarded by the Adjudicator and enforced by way of summary judgment) at the end of the substantive trial, or arbitration hearing, may constitute special circumstances within the meaning of Order 47 rule 1(1)(a) rendering it appropriate to grant a stay (see *Herschel*).

e) If the claimant is in insolvent liquidation, or there is no dispute on the evidence that the claimant is insolvent, then a stay of execution will usually be granted (see *Bouygues* and *Rainford House*).

f) Even if the evidence of the claimant's present financial position suggested that it is probable that it would be unable to repay the judgment sum when it fell due, that would not usually justify the grant of a stay if:

  (i) the claimant's financial position is the same or similar to its financial position at the time that the relevant contract was made (see *Herschel*); or

  (ii) the claimant's financial position is due, either wholly, or in significant part, to the defendant's failure to pay those sums which were awarded by the adjudicator (see *Absolute Rentals*).'

Applying these principles to the facts of the case the judge concluded that the defendant had not demonstrated that the claimant would be unable to pay the sums back in any future arbitration and that in any event the claimant's financial position had significantly changed from the date on which it was made, and further that any financial problems of the claimant being relied upon by the defendant were largely the defendant's own fault by failing to pay the sums eventually awarded by the adjudicator.

See also *Total M&E Services Ltd v ABB Technologies Ltd* (2002), summarised at 5.1, in which ABB sought a stay of execution on the basis of the impecuniosity of the claimant. The judge concluded that the claimant had few fixed assets but that the evidence as to the risk of future non-payment was not based on compelling and uncontradicted evidence. He therefore concluded that there were no special circumstances that rendered it inexpedient to enforce the judgment.

See also *S. L. Timber Systems Ltd v Carillion Construction Ltd* (2001), summarised at 10.2, in which the judge was reluctant to apply the reasoning in English decisions and concluded that Carillion's assertions to the effect that S. L. Timber were insolvent did not constitute a relevant defence.

11.4 POTENTIAL COUNTERCLAIMS

The decision of an adjudicator will usually be enforced even if there is a potential counterclaim.

Macob Civil Engineering Ltd v Morrison Construction Ltd (1999)

This was the first case in which the court had an opportunity to consider the adjudication provisions of the Act. Macob were ground works contractors; they entered into a contract with Morrison to carry out ground works at a retail development in Wales. Disputes arose with regard to an interim application for payment, which Macob referred to adjudication. The adjudicator decided that Morrison should pay Macob the sum of £302,366.34 plus VAT, plus interest and the adjudicator's fees.

Morrison did not comply with this decision and Macob sought to enforce it in court.

Morrison defended the application on the basis that they were challenging the adjudicator's decision, which was therefore not enforceable; and also that the contract contained a valid arbitration clause.

With regard to the first point, the judge concluded that a decision in respect of which the validity is challenged is nevertheless a decision within the meaning of the Act and is therefore enforceable.

With regard to the arbitration clause, the judge refused to accept that just because the dispute was subject to a separate reference to arbitration the decision of the adjudicator should not be enforced.

The judge therefore gave a declaration in favour of Macob.

F W Cook Ltd v Shimizu (UK) Ltd (2000)

Cook were subcontractors to Shimizu for mechanical works in relation to a building project in the London Docklands. Disputes arose after completion of the works in relation to a number of items in the final account. Cook referred some of these to adjudication.

The adjudicator decided that certain sums were payable, but the parties disagreed as to what this meant: Cook interpreted the adjudicator's decision as requiring Shimizu to pay the stated sums within the stated period; however, Shimizu interpreted the adjudicator's decision as requiring it to make provision within the final account for the stated sums in respect of the stated items.

Cook immediately issued proceedings and made an application for summary judgment. The judge found that Shimizu had a realistic prospect of success in demonstrating that its interpretation of the adjudicator's decision was correct.

The judge went on to say that if Shimizu's interpretation was not correct, then the adjudicator had exceeded his jurisdiction as the notice of referral to adjudication had not asked him to decide that which Cook now argued he had in fact decided.

VHE Construction plc v RBSTB Trust Co Ltd (2000)

VHE had entered into a construction contract with RBSTB under the JCT standard form of building contract with contractor's design. The contract provided that if RBSTB should fail to issue a payment notice within five days of receipt of an application for payment, the contractor shall be entitled to be paid the sum applied for.

VHE made two applications for payment totalling £1,037,898.05, in respect of which RBSTB failed to serve any payment notices or withholding notices – nor did they pay the sum applied for.

This matter was the subject of two separate adjudications. In the first adjudication, the adjudicator decided that VHE were entitled to the sum applied for, namely £1,037,898.05. In the second adjudication, the adjudicator decided that he had the power to open up, review and revise the sum due to the contractor, and he reduced the amount due to £207,857.14 plus interest.

VHE issued an invoice in respect of the sum found to due by the first adjudicator in respect of which RBSTB failed to issue any withholding notices. RBSTB meanwhile claimed that it had an entitlement to liquidated damages, which reduced the sum payable pursuant to the decision of the second adjudicator to £46,974.69. This sum was duly paid.

Before looking at the issue of liquidated damages the judge concluded that the effect of the two decisions was that VHE were entitled to be paid the sum found due by the first adjudicator but became liable to repay the difference between that and the sum found due by the second adjudicator on the publication of the second adjudicator's decision.

With regard to the attempt by RBSTB to deduct liquidated damages, the judge found that there was no provision in the contract entitling RBSTB to deduct liquidated damages from the adjudicator's award, but on the contrary the contract required RBSTB to comply with the decision of the adjudicator. This, the judge found, meant comply without recourse to defences or cross-claims not raised in the adjudication.

The judge therefore concluded that RBSTB had no real prospect of successfully defending the claim by VHE and therefore gave summary judgement against it.

David McLean Housing Contractors Ltd v Swansea Housing Association Ltd (2001)

Essentially the issues between the parties in this matter were whether the claimant contractor was to be paid an amount of liquidated damages to which the defendant employer considered that it was entitled.

The issue arose out of an adjudication that had been referred by the contractor. The notice of intention to adjudicate contained six heads of claim, including the contractor's entitlement to loss and expense and extensions of time, but did not include a reference to liquidated damages.

On production of the adjudicator's decision the employer issued a notice of intention to deduct the liquidated damages, taking into account the adjudicator's decision as to extensions of time.

The judge held that the defendant had a realistic prospect of success in demonstrating that the notice of intention to deduct liquidated damages was a valid withholding notice against the adjudicator's decision. However, even if he was wrong on this point, the judge concluded that the liquidated damages raised by way of counterclaim in the application for summary judgment was a viable counterclaim. No defence to it had been raised and there was no realistic prospect available to the claimant for resisting payment on that counterclaim.

Therefore the judge refused the claimant's application for summary judgment as the defendant had realistic prospects of success.

Bovis Lend Lease Ltd v Triangle Development Ltd (2002)

Bovis entered into a management contract with Triangle to refurbish and fit out three existing Victorian schoolhouses into 43 luxury residential apartments. Disputes arose as to the valuation of two interim certificates, which Bovis referred to adjudication. Triangle counter-adjudicated with two further notices of adjudication. Bovis then argued that Triangle were in repudiatory breach and sought to accept that repudiatory breach as terminating their employment under the contract. Triangle also served notice terminating Bovis's employment under the contract.

The first adjudication concerning the two interim certificates was issued on 12 September 2002 and concluded that Triangle should pay Bovis £158,000 with interest. The decision in the second adjudication was given on 13 September 2002, in which the adjudicator decided that Bovis was in breach of its contractual obligations by not providing certain of the documents required by Triangle. The decision in the third adjudication was given on 26 September 2002 and was to the effect that Triangle were not in repudiatory breach and the contract had therefore not been brought to an end by Bovis's attempted acceptance of Triangle's alleged repudiatory breach.

All of these matters came before the court by way of an application by Bovis for a declaration that Triangle were liable to pay the sums decided by the adjudicator in the first adjudication. Triangle resisted this application on the basis of the adjudicator's subsequent decisions.

The judge concluded that the first and third adjudication decisions were in conflict, which had arisen because the parties had chosen to refer their existing dispute piecemeal to adjudication. As a result, there were two conflicting decisions, one giving Bovis a right to payment and the other giving Triangle the right to cross-claim and to liquidated damages flowing from Bovis's repudiation of the contract. It was not possible, in these proceedings, to determine whether Triangle's cross-claim was sufficient to defeat or merely reduce Bovis's claim, but Triangle also claimed an entitlement to rely on a provision of the contract that provided that, following determination of the contractor's employment, the provisions of the contract requiring further payments to be made were not to apply.

The judge concluded that where there were contractual terms that clearly have the effect of suspending or providing that an entitlement to avoid or deduct from a payment directed to be paid by the adjudicator's decision, those terms will prevail. Equally, where a paying party is given an entitlement to deduct from, or cross-claim against, the sum directed to be paid as a result of the same, or another adjudication decision, the first decision will not be enforced or, alternatively, judgment will be stayed. Therefore, the judge concluded that Triangle were entitled to rely on the provision of the contract that suspended payment of further sums, even those directed to be paid pursuant to the adjudicator's first decision.

[Note that this case was decided before the Court of Appeal decision in *Ferson v Levolux* (2003), summarised at 1.10.]

Guardi Shoes Ltd v Datum Contracts (2002)

Datum entered into a contract with Guardi for the refurbishment and fitting out of a shop that Guardi intended to open. There remained some snagging items for which Datum accepted responsibility and was prepared to return and attend to at its own expense. However, Guardi took the view that the defects were substantial and that it had lost confidence in Datum and was not prepared to have Datum do any more work. Guardi sought to withhold money against Datum and Datum referred the dispute to adjudication. Guardi had failed to serve the appropriate withholding notices in respect of the defects, and so the adjudicator found that Datum was entitled to be paid the balance of what was due to it under the contract.

Datum sought to enforce the adjudicator's decision and succeeded in obtaining judgment in its favour.

Guardi made part-payment against the sum due, but eventually were presented with a winding-up petition. Guardi then commenced this application to prevent Datum from advertising that petition.

During the application to prevent Datum from advertising the petition, Guardi raised its cross-claim in respect of defects that it claimed equalled or exceeded the outstanding amount due to Datum. In order to succeed, Guardi were required to demonstrate that they were unable to litigate the amount of the cross-claim previously.

The judge concluded that Guardi had the opportunity to serve an appropriate counter-notice under the terms of the contract but they failed to take it. Guardi had come before the court saying, in effect, that although they hadn't operated the machinery under which their obligation to pay would be put into suspense, Datum should be left in the same practical position as if Guardi had operated that machinery. Datum proceeded to judgment. It had now taken the step that is quite usual, for an unsatisfied judgment creditor, in presenting a petition.

In all the circumstances of this case the judge concluded that Guardi only had itself to blame. Its position was weak. The presentation of a petition in the circumstances of this case was not an abuse. The petition was certainly not bound to be dismissed if it proceeded. In those circumstances, the judge refused the application.

Solland International Ltd v Daraydan Holdings Ltd (2002)

Solland were building contractors undertaking construction work on behalf of Daraydan. Disputes arose with regard to payment of an interim certificate, which Solland referred to adjudication. The adjudicator found that the certified sums were payable, but Daraydan continued to resist payment.

These proceedings were brought by Solland to enforce the adjudicator's decision, and they applied for summary judgment. The application for summary judgment was resisted by Daraydan on the basis that they had a cross-claim for liquidated damages that exceeded the amount of Solland's claim in the action.

The judge concluded that the sum that the adjudicator had determined to be paid became payable under the contract, notwithstanding that the determination was itself a decision as to what sum was payable under the contract. Consequently, in the ordinary case, as there will be no notice of intention to withhold payment of some amount of what an adjudicator determined to be due, there can be no question but that the amount that the adjudicator decides is due is payable in full.

In this case, as a result of the decision of the adjudicator, Daraydan became obliged under the terms of the building contract, including the terms of the Scheme as incorporated therein, to pay Solland the sum of £658,944.72 plus interest and the adjudicator's fee. Solland were entitled to judgment.

The Construction Centre Group Ltd v The Highland Council (2003)

The Construction Centre Group entered into a contract with the Highland Council for the construction of an island ferry scheme based on the Institution of Civil Engineers (ICE) standard form of contract (5th edition). A dispute arose between the parties as to the Construction Centre Group's entitlement pursuant to an interim application for payment. The Construction Centre Group referred this dispute to adjudication. The adjudicator decided that a sum of £245,469.24 was payable by the Highland Council to the Construction Centre Group.

The Highland Council failed to pay, so the Construction Centre Group commenced proceedings to enforce the adjudicator's decision.

The Highland Council sought to resist enforcement of the adjudicator's decision and made its own claim on the basis that it was entitled to a sum of £420,000 as liquidated damages for delay.

There was some dispute as to whether the adjudicator was, or might have been, seized of jurisdiction to determine the employer's entitlement to liquidated damages, but it was accepted that the Highland Council could, if it had seen fit, have relied on this claim before the adjudicator. The court concluded that because the contra-debt for liquidated damages had not been relied upon as it might have been before the adjudicator, the Highland Council could not, consistent with its contractual obligations to give effect forthwith to the adjudicator's award, now plead compensation on the basis of that contra-debt. The Highland Council, having allowed the adjudicator's order to pass against it when it might have pled an admissible contra-debt in answer is, by virtue of its contractual obligation to give effect forthwith to that decision, precluded from pleading in the judicial action of enforcement compensation on the basis of that contra-debt.

Dumarc Building Services Ltd v Mr Salvador Rico (2003)

This case concerned work to the home of a residential occupier. Therefore the Act did not apply. However, the JCT contract that had been executed between the parties had been amended so that the contractual adjudication provisions applied to these works.

The employer sought to withhold money by way of liquidated damages for delay from a payment certificate issued by the architect. The contractor disputed the employer's right to do so and referred the dispute to adjudication.

The adjudicator found that a lesser sum than that certified was due to the contractor and ordered that payment be made accordingly. The employer did not make payment in accordance with the adjudicator's decision, and therefore Durmac sought to enforce the decision by way of an application for summary judgement.

Having failed to have their claim for liquidated damages properly addressed by the adjudicator, the employer sought to raise the argument again as a defence to the application for summary judgment.

Following the Court of Appeal's decision in *Levolux v Ferson* (2003) (summarised at 1.10) the judge welcomed the simplification of the law and entered judgment for the applicant.

William Verry Ltd v North West London Communal Mikvah (2004)

William Verry were contractors for the construction of a Jewish ritual bath. A number of disputes arose during the course of the works, which William Verry referred to adjudication on several occasions.

In the last adjudication, NWLCM failed to pay in accordance with the adjudicator's decision and William Verry applied for summary judgment. NWLCM resisted the application on three grounds:

(1) They argued that the referral notice was served one day too late.

(2) They argued that there was no dispute in existence when William Verry served its notice of adjudication.

(3) They argued that the adjudicator had failed to consider an issue that had been referred to him.

With regard to point (1), the judge concluded that the Act requires that the contractual timescale should have the object of securing the referral of the dispute to the adjudicator within seven days of the adjudication notice. Thus, the statute is setting a minimum requirement for the contract. The contract must allow a referring party, if it chooses, to issue a referral notice within the prescribed seven-day timescale. However, there is nothing in the Act to preclude the contract from being drafted so as to provide additional machinery that enables the adjudicator to extend that timescale and enable the referring party to refer the dispute outside the seven-day period if it chooses to. In other words, the Act requires contractual machinery that enables the referring party to refer the dispute within seven days of the adjudication notice, but it does not prohibit a machinery that additionally enables the referring party to refer the dispute outside that timescale if it elects to take longer in making the reference.

Therefore, in the light of William Verry's compliance with the adjudicator's procedural direction as to the service of the referral notice, that notice was served within time and the subsequent adjudication and the resultant decision of the adjudicator was not invalidated by the referral notice being served out of time.

With regard to point (2), the judge concluded that the nil valuation that had been referred to adjudication was the culmination of a lengthy and contentious process that had started when William Verry had contended that the works were both satisfactorily complete and that practical completion had been achieved, whereas NWLCM's agent had asserted that the works contained significant defects that precluded them from being regarded as complete or as having achieved practical completion. The judge therefore concluded that the adjudication notice referred an existing dispute that had already crystallised to adjudication. The notice was not premature and the adjudicator was validly appointed.

With regard to point (3), the judge concluded that the adjudicator had made several errors, most notably in failing to take into account arguments of abatement raised by NWLCM. The question was whether the errors of law were errors made within jurisdiction or were so fundamental that their effect was to transform the adjudicator's consideration of the referred question or dispute into a consideration and determination of a different question or dispute to the referred question. On balance, the judge concluded that the errors of the adjudicator were made as part of his answering the right question wrongly, rather than in answering the wrong question.

Having concluded that the adjudicator failed to take into account arguments of abatement that had been properly referred to him, the judge was reluctant to enforce the adjudicator's decision, which would require payment. However, that was the logical effect of the judge's earlier finding that the adjudicator had answered the right question wrongly and his decision was therefore made within jurisdiction.

The judge therefore decided that the adjudicator's decision should be enforced, but that the judgment should not to be drawn up for six weeks from the date of handing down so as to give NWLCM sufficient time to commence another adjudication on the abatement point. If that subsequent adjudication decision is in favour of NWLCM, effect can then be given to those developments so that one decision can be set against the other and only that balancing figure paid to the net winner.

See also *A & D Maintenance and Construction Ltd v Pagehurst Construction Services Ltd* (2000), summarised at 1.10, in which it was unsuccessfully argued before the court that as there were other ongoing proceedings to recover losses sustained by reason of a fire, the application for summary judgment to enforce the adjudicator's decision should be dismissed. The court concluded that it would not have been disposed to give leave to defend the enforcement proceedings in the absence of other proceedings. Further, that adjudication is a remarkable and possibly unique intervention whereby the ordinary freedom of contract between commercial parties to regulate their relationships has been overridden and that the intention of parliament is clear – that disputes are to go to adjudication and the decision of the adjudicator has to be complied with, pending final determination.

However, see also *Shimizu Europe Ltd v LBJ Fabrications Ltd* (2003), summarised at 2.4, in which the judge, considering the contractual mechanism for payment, concluded that the adjudicator did what Shimizu should have done, which was to value the work properly. The contract required that sum to be invoiced before payment became due. Therefore the perform-ance of the valuation function did not deprive Shimizu of its subsequent rights to withhold sums from the invoiced amount.

11.5 MEANS OF ENFORCEMENT

The appropriate means to enforce decisions of adjudicators will usually be via an application for summary judgment.

Absolute Rentals Ltd v Gencor Enterprises Ltd (1999)

In this case the claimants were seeking summary judgment to enforce the decision of an adjudicator in respect of works undertaken by them for the defendant.

One of the arguments raised by the defendants was that the contract contained an arbitration clause and therefore the court proceedings should be stayed to arbitration. The court concluded that on this claim the defendant had no defence and therefore gave summary judgment to the claimants.

Outwing Construction Ltd v Randall & Son Ltd (1999)

Outwing were groundworks subcontractors undertaking works for Randall under the terms of DOM/1. Disputes arose as to the valuation of the final account. Outwing referred this dispute to adjudication and the adjudicator decided that Outwing should be paid the sum that they had applied for, in addition to the adjudicator's fee, the total amount due being £16,096.98.

Randall failed to pay the sum found due by the adjudicator within the timescale laid down by the adjudicator, so Outwing sought to enforce the decision in court and applied for summary judgement.

Prior to the hearing Randall paid the principal sum outstanding, but the parties could not agree on liability for legal costs. The matter therefore proceeded on the basis of costs only.

Outwing had successfully applied for an abridgement of the usual court timescale to bring this matter before the court unusually quickly. Randall had argued that Outwing were unjustified in doing so and that therefore Outwing were liable to pay Randall's additional costs incurred as a result.

The judge concluded that the issue of a summons to abridge time was justified. Action to enforce an adjudicator's decision is not comparable to the ordinary process of recovering an apparently undisputed debt. However, he did go on to say that it might not be appropriate to abridge time in every case.

The judge therefore found in favour of Outwing.

George Parke v The Fenton Gretton Partnership (2000)

Parke appointed Fenton as contractors to refurbish a bar in which he had a leasehold interest. Fenton sought payment of their final account – the sum of £169,269 – but Parke argued that the work had not been finished, that there were snagging works to do and that there had been delays.

Fenton referred the dispute to adjudication. The adjudicator made his decision in favour of Fenton, awarding them the full amount of their claim plus interest and VAT. Parke failed to pay, so Fenton served a statutory demand.

Parke failed to respond to that statutory demand and subsequently applied to have it set aside.

The judge held that the adjudication created a debt that may form the basis of a statutory demand. It falls to be treated in the same way as a judgment or order and the courts will not go behind it. However, on the basis that a separate action was proceeding in the Technology and Construction Court and failure to set aside the statutory demand could result in the bankruptcy of Parke, the judge agreed to set aside the statutory demand.

See also *Workplace Technologies plc v E Squared Ltd and Mr J. L. Riches* (2000), summarised at 1.1, in which in response to an application for an injunction to restrain the referring party from continuing with the adjudication the judge concluded that he was not persuaded that there is power to grant an injunction to restrain a party initiating a void reference and pursuing proceedings that themselves are void and that may give rise to a void, and thus unenforceable, adjudication decision. There does not appear to be any legal or equitable interest such as an injunction would protect. Doubtless the initiation of such proceedings may be conceived to be a source of harassment, pressure or needless expense.

Appendix 1
Housing Grants, Construction and Regeneration Act 1996, sections 104–108

104. Construction contracts

(1) In this Part a 'construction contract' means an agreement with a person for any of the following –

(a) the carrying out of construction operations;

(b) arranging for the carrying out of construction operations by others, whether under sub-contract to him or otherwise;

(c) providing his own labour, or the labour of others, for the carrying out of construction operations.

(2) References in this Part to a construction contract include an agreement –

(a) to do architectural, design, or surveying work, or

(b) to provide advice on building, engineering, interior or exterior decoration or on the laying-out of landscape,

in relation to construction operations.

(3) References in this Part to a construction contract do not include a contract of employment (within the meaning of the Employment Rights Act 1996).

(4) The Secretary of State may by order add to, amend or repeal any of the provisions of subsection (1), (2) or (3) as to the agreements which are construction contracts for the purposes of this Part or are to be taken or not to be taken as included in references to such contracts.

No such order shall be made unless a draft of it has been laid before and approved by a resolution of each House of Parliament.

(5) Where an agreement relates to construction operations and other matters, this Part applies to it only so far as it relates to construction operations.

An agreement relates to construction operations so far as it makes provision of any kind within subsection (1) or (2).

(6) This Part applies only to construction contracts which –

(a) are entered into after the commencement of this Part, and
(b) relate to the carrying out of construction operations in England, Wales or Scotland.

(7) This Part applies whether or not the law of England and Wales or Scotland is otherwise the applicable law in relation to the contract.

105. Meaning of 'construction operations'

(1) In this Part 'construction operations' means, subject as follows, operations of any of the following descriptions –

(a) construction, alteration, repair, maintenance, extension, demolition or dismantling of buildings, or structures forming, or to form, part of the land (whether permanent or not);

(b) construction, alteration, repair, maintenance, extension, demolition or dismantling of any works forming, or to form, part of the land, including (without prejudice to the foregoing) walls, roadworks, power-lines, tele-communication apparatus, aircraft runways, docks and harbours, railways, inland waterways, pipe-lines, reservoirs, water-mains, wells, sewers, industrial plant and installations for purposes of land drainage, coast protection or defence;

(c) installation in any building or structure of fittings forming part of the land, including (without prejudice to the foregoing) systems of heating, lighting, air-conditioning, ventilation, power supply, drainage, sanitation, water supply or fire protection, or security or communications systems;

(d) external or internal cleaning of buildings and structures, so far as carried out in the course of their construction, alteration, repair, extension or restoration;

(e) operations which form an integral part of, or are preparatory to, or are for rendering complete, such operations as are previously described in this subsection, including site clearance, earth-moving, excavation, tunnelling and boring, laying of foundations, erection, maintenance or dismantling of scaffolding, site restoration, landscaping and the provision of roadways and other access works;

(f) painting or decorating the internal or external surfaces of any building or structure.

(2) The following operations are not construction operations within the meaning of this Part –

(a) drilling for, or extraction of, oil or natural gas;

(b) extraction (whether by underground or surface working) of minerals; tunnelling or boring, or construction of underground works, for this purpose;

(c) assembly, installation or demolition of plant or machinery, or erection or demolition of steelwork for the purposes of supporting or providing access to plant or machinery, on a site where the primary activity is –
    (i) nuclear processing, power generation, or water or effluent treatment, or
    (ii) the production, transmission, processing or bulk storage (other than warehousing) of chemicals, pharmaceuticals, oil, gas, steel or food and drink;

(d) manufacture or delivery to site of –
    (i) building or engineering components or equipment,
    (ii) materials, plant or machinery, or
    (iii) components for systems of heating, lighting, air-conditioning, ventilation, power supply, drainage, sanitation, water supply or fire protection, or for security or communications systems,
    except under a contract which also provides for their installation;

(e) the making, installation, and repair of artistic works, being sculptures, murals and other works which are wholly artistic in nature.

(3) The Secretary of State may by order add to, amend or repeal any of the provisions of subsection (1) or (2) as to the operations and work to be treated as construction operations for the purposes of this Part.

(4) No such order shall be made unless a draft of it has been laid before and approved by a resolution of each House of Parliament.

106. Provisions not applicable to contract with residential occupier

(1) This Part does not apply –

(a) to a construction contract with a residential occupier (see below), or

(b) to any other description of construction contract excluded from the operation of this Part by order of the Secretary of State.

(2) A construction contract with a residential occupier means a construction contract which principally relates to operations on a dwelling which one of the parties to the contract occupies, or intends to occupy, as his residence.

In this subsection 'dwelling' means a dwelling-house or a flat; and for this purpose –

'dwelling-house' does not include a building containing a flat; and
'flat' means separate and self-contained premises constructed or adapted for use for residential purposes and forming part of a building from some other part of which the premises are divided horizontally.

(3) The Secretary of State may by order amend subsection (2).

(4) No order under this section shall be made unless a draft of it has been laid before and approved by a resolution of each House of Parliament.

107. Provisions applicable only to agreements in writing

(1) The provisions of this Part apply only where the construction contract is in writing, and any other agreement between the parties as to any matter is effective for the purposes of this Part only if in writing.

The expressions 'agreement', 'agree' and 'agreed' shall be construed accordingly.

(2) There is an agreement in writing –

(a) if the agreement is made in writing (whether or not it is signed by the parties),
(b) if the agreement is made by exchange of communications in writing, or
(c) if the agreement is evidenced in writing.

(3) Where parties agree otherwise than in writing by reference to terms which are in writing, they make an agreement in writing.

(4) An agreement is evidenced in writing if an agreement made otherwise than in writing is recorded by one of the parties, or by a third party, with the authority of the parties to the agreement.

(5) An exchange of written submissions in adjudication proceedings, or in arbitral or legal proceedings in which the existence of an agreement otherwise than in writing is alleged by one party against another party and not denied by the other party in his response constitutes as between those parties an agreement in writing to the effect alleged.

(6) References in this Part to anything being written or in writing include its being recorded by any means.

108. Right to refer disputes to adjudication

(1) A party to a construction contract has the right to refer a dispute arising under the contract for adjudication under a procedure complying with this section.
For this purpose 'dispute' includes any difference.

(2) The contract shall –

(a) enable a party to give notice at any time of his intention to refer a dispute to adjudication;
(b) provide a timetable with the object of securing the appointment of the adjudicator and referral of the dispute to him within 7 days of such notice;
(c) require the adjudicator to reach a decision within 28 days of referral or such longer period as is agreed by the parties after the dispute has been referred;

(d) allow the adjudicator to extend the period of 28 days by up to 14 days, with the consent of the party by whom the dispute was referred;

(e) impose a duty on the adjudicator to act impartially; and

(f) enable the adjudicator to take the initiative in ascertaining the facts and the law.

(3) The contract shall provide that the decision of the adjudicator is binding until the dispute is finally determined by legal proceedings, by arbitration (if the contract provides for arbitration or the parties otherwise agree to arbitration) or by agreement.

The parties may agree to accept the decision of the adjudicator as finally determining the dispute.

(4) The contract shall also provide that the adjudicator is not liable for anything done or omitted in the discharge or purported discharge of his functions as adjudicator unless the act or omission is in bad faith, and that any employee or agent of the adjudicator is similarly protected from liability.

(5) If the contract does not comply with the requirements of subsections (1) to (4), the adjudication provisions of the Scheme for Construction Contracts apply.

(6) For England and Wales, the Scheme may apply the provisions of the Arbitration Act 1996 with such adaptations and modifications as appear to the Minister making the scheme to be appropriate.

For Scotland, the Scheme may include provision conferring powers on courts in relation to adjudication and provision relating to the enforcement of the adjudicator's decision.

Crown copyright material is reproduced with the permission of the Controller of HMSO and the Queen's Printer for Scotland.

Appendix 2
Scheme for Construction Contracts (England and Wales) Regulations 1998

SI 1998 No 649

CONSTRUCTION, ENGLAND AND WALES

The Scheme for Construction Contracts (England and Wales) Regulations 1998

Made	*6th March 1998*
Coming into force	*1st May 1998*

The Secretary of State, in exercise of the powers conferred on him by sections 108(6), 114 and 146(1) and (2) of the Housing Grants, Construction and Regeneration Act 1996, and of all other powers enabling him in that behalf, having consulted such persons as he thinks fit, and draft Regulations having been approved by both Houses of Parliament, hereby makes the following Regulations:

Citation, commencement, extent and interpretation

1. – (1) These Regulations may be cited as the Scheme for Construction Contracts (England and Wales) Regulations 1998 and shall come into force at the end of the period of 8 weeks beginning with the day on which they are made (the 'commencement date').

(2) These Regulations shall extend only to England and Wales.

(3) In these Regulations, 'the Act' means the Housing Grants, Construction and Regeneration Act 1996.

The Scheme for Construction Contracts

2. Where a construction contract does not comply with the requirements of section 108(1) to (4) of the Act, the adjudication provisions in Part I of the Schedule to these Regulations shall apply.

3. Where–

(a) the parties to a construction contract are unable to reach agreement for the purposes mentioned respectively in sections 109, 111 and 113 of the Act, or

(b) a construction contract does not make provision as required by section 110 of the Act,

the relevant provisions in Part II of the Schedule to these Regulations shall apply.

4. The provisions in the Schedule to these Regulations shall be the Scheme for Construction Contracts for the purposes of section 114 of the Act.

Signed by authority of the Secretary of State

Nick Raynsford

Parliamentary Under-Secretary of State, Department of the Environment, Transport and the Regions

6th March 1998

SCHEDULE

Regulations 2, 3 and 4

THE SCHEME FOR CONSTRUCTION CONTRACTS

PART I – ADJUDICATION

Notice of Intention to seek Adjudication

1. – (1) Any party to a construction contract (the 'referring party') may give written notice (the 'notice of adjudication') of his intention to refer any dispute arising under the contract, to adjudication.

(2) The notice of adjudication shall be given to every other party to the contract.

(3) The notice of adjudication shall set out briefly–

(a) the nature and a brief description of the dispute and of the parties involved,
(b) details of where and when the dispute has arisen,
(c) the nature of the redress which is sought, and
(d) the names and addresses of the parties to the contract (including, where appropriate, the addresses which the parties have specified for the giving of notices).

2. – (1) Following the giving of a notice of adjudication and subject to any agreement between the parties to the dispute as to who shall act as adjudicator–

(a) the referring party shall request the person (if any) specified in the contract to act as adjudicator, or
(b) if no person is named in the contract or the person named has already indicated that he is unwilling or unable to act, and the contract provides for a specified nominating body to select a person, the referring party shall request the nominating body named in the contract to select a person to act as adjudicator, or
(c) where neither paragraph (a) nor (b) above applies, or where the person referred to in (a) has already indicated that he is unwilling or unable to act and (b) does not apply, the referring party shall request an adjudicator nominating body to select a person to act as adjudicator.

(2) A person requested to act as adjudicator in accordance with the provisions of paragraph (1) shall indicate whether or not he is willing to act within two days of receiving the request.

(3) In this paragraph, and in paragraphs 5 and 6 below, an 'adjudicator nominating body' shall mean a body (not being a natural person and not being a party to the dispute) which holds itself out publicly as a body which will select an adjudicator when requested to do so by a referring party.

3. The request referred to in paragraphs 2, 5 and 6 shall be accompanied by a copy of the notice of adjudication.

4. Any person requested or selected to act as adjudicator in accordance with paragraphs 2, 5 or 6 shall be a natural person acting in his personal capacity. A person requested or selected to act as an adjudicator shall not be an employee of any of the parties to the dispute and shall declare any interest, financial or otherwise, in any matter relating to the dispute.

5. – (1) The nominating body referred to in paragraphs 2(1)(b) and 6(1)(b) or the adjudicator nominating body referred to in paragraphs 2(1)(c), 5(2)(b) and 6(1)(c) must communicate the selection of an adjudicator to the referring party within five days of receiving a request to do so.

(2) Where the nominating body or the adjudicator nominating body fails to comply with paragraph (1), the referring party may–

(a) agree with the other party to the dispute to request a specified person to act as adjudicator, or

(b) request any other adjudicator nominating body to select a person to act as adjudicator.

(3) The person requested to act as adjudicator in accordance with the provisions of paragraphs (1) or (2) shall indicate whether or not he is willing to act within two days of receiving the request.

6. – (1) Where an adjudicator who is named in the contract indicates to the parties that he is unable or unwilling to act, or where he fails to respond in accordance with paragraph 2(2), the referring party may–

(a) request another person (if any) specified in the contract to act as adjudicator, or

(b) request the nominating body (if any) referred to in the contract to select a person to act as adjudicator, or

(c) request any other adjudicator nominating body to select a person to act as adjudicator.

(2) The person requested to act in accordance with the provisions of paragraph (1) shall indicate whether or not he is willing to act within two days of receiving the request.

7. – (1) Where an adjudicator has been selected in accordance with paragraphs 2, 5 or 6, the referring party shall, not later than seven days from the date of the notice of adjudication, refer the dispute in writing (the 'referral notice') to the adjudicator.

(2) A referral notice shall be accompanied by copies of, or relevant extracts from, the construction contract and such other documents as the referring party intends to rely upon.

(3) The referring party shall, at the same time as he sends to the adjudicator the documents referred to in paragraphs (1) and (2), send copies of those documents to every other party to the dispute.

8. – (1) The adjudicator may, with the consent of all the parties to those disputes, adjudicate at the same time on more than one dispute under the same contract.

(2) The adjudicator may, with the consent of all the parties to those disputes, adjudicate at the same time on related disputes under different contracts, whether or not one or more of those parties is a party to those disputes.

(3) All the parties in paragraphs (1) and (2) respectively may agree to extend the period within which the adjudicator may reach a decision in relation to all or any of these disputes.

(4) Where an adjudicator ceases to act because a dispute is to be adjudicated on by another person in terms of this paragraph, that adjudicator's fees and expenses shall be determined in accordance with paragraph 25.

9. – (1) An adjudicator may resign at any time on giving notice in writing to the parties to the dispute.

(2) An adjudicator must resign where the dispute is the same or substantially the same as one which has previously been referred to adjudication, and a decision has been taken in that adjudication.

(3) Where an adjudicator ceases to act under paragraph 9(1)–

(a) the referring party may serve a fresh notice under paragraph 1 and shall request an adjudicator to act in accordance with paragraphs 2 to 7; and

(b) if requested by the new adjudicator and insofar as it is reasonably practicable, the parties shall supply him with copies of all documents which they had made available to the previous adjudicator.

(4) Where an adjudicator resigns in the circumstances referred to in paragraph (2), or where a dispute varies significantly from the dispute referred to him in the referral notice and for that reason he is not competent to decide it, the adjudicator shall be entitled to the payment of such reasonable amount as he may determine by way of fees and expenses reasonably incurred by him. The parties shall be jointly and severally liable for any sum which remains outstanding following the making of any determination on how the payment shall be apportioned.

10. Where any party to the dispute objects to the appointment of a particular person as adjudicator, that objection shall not invalidate the adjudicator's appointment nor any decision he may reach in accordance with paragraph 20.

11. – (1) The parties to a dispute may at any time agree to revoke the appointment of the adjudicator. The adjudicator shall be entitled to the payment of such reasonable amount as he may determine by way of fees and expenses incurred by him. The parties shall be jointly and severally liable for any sum which remains outstanding following the making of any determination on how the payment shall be apportioned.

(2) Where the revocation of the appointment of the adjudicator is due to the default or misconduct of the adjudicator, the parties shall not be liable to pay the adjudicator's fees and expenses.

Powers of the adjudicator

12. The adjudicator shall–

(a) act impartially in carrying out his duties and shall do so in accordance with any relevant terms of the contract and shall reach his decision in accordance with the applicable law in relation to the contract; and

(b) avoid incurring unnecessary expense.

13. The adjudicator may take the initiative in ascertaining the facts and the law necessary to determine the dispute, and shall decide on the procedure to be followed in the adjudication. In particular he may–

(a) request any party to the contract to supply him with such documents as he may reasonably require including, if he so directs, any written statement from any party to the contract supporting or supplementing the referral notice and any other documents given under paragraph 7(2),

(b) decide the language or languages to be used in the adjudication and whether a translation of any document is to be provided and if so by whom,

(c) meet and question any of the parties to the contract and their representatives,

(d) subject to obtaining any necessary consent from a third party or parties, make such site visits and inspections as he considers appropriate, whether accompanied by the parties or not,

(e) subject to obtaining any necessary consent from a third party or parties, carry out any tests or experiments,

(f) obtain and consider such representations and submissions as he requires, and, provided he has notified the parties of his intention, appoint experts, assessors or legal advisers,

(g) give directions as to the timetable for the adjudication, any deadlines, or limits as to the length of written documents or oral representations to be complied with, and

(h) issue other directions relating to the conduct of the adjudication.

14. The parties shall comply with any request or direction of the adjudicator in relation to the adjudication.

15. If, without showing sufficient cause, a party fails to comply with any request, direction or timetable of the adjudicator made in accordance with his powers, fails to produce any document or written statement requested by the adjudicator, or in any other way fails to comply with a requirement under these provisions relating to the adjudication, the adjudicator may–

(a) continue the adjudication in the absence of that party or of the document or written statement requested,

(b) draw such inferences from that failure to comply as circumstances may, in the adjudicator's opinion, be justified, and

(c) make a decision on the basis of the information before him attaching such weight as he thinks fit to any evidence submitted to him outside any period he may have requested or directed.

16. – (1) Subject to any agreement between the parties to the contrary, and to the terms of paragraph (2) below, any party to the dispute may be assisted by, or represented by, such advisers or representatives (whether legally qualified or not) as he considers appropriate.

(2) Where the adjudicator is considering oral evidence or representations, a party to the dispute may not be represented by more than one person, unless the adjudicator gives directions to the contrary.

17. The adjudicator shall consider any relevant information submitted to him by any of the parties to the dispute and shall make available to them any information to be taken into account in reaching his decision.

18. The adjudicator and any party to the dispute shall not disclose to any other person any information or document provided to him in connection with the adjudication which the party supplying it has indicated is to be treated as confidential, except to the extent that it is necessary for the purposes of, or in connection with, the adjudication.

19. – (1) The adjudicator shall reach his decision not later than–

(a) twenty eight days after the date of the referral notice mentioned in paragraph 7(1), or

(b) forty two days after the date of the referral notice if the referring party so consents, or

(c) such period exceeding twenty eight days after the referral notice as the parties to the dispute may, after the giving of that notice, agree.

(2) Where the adjudicator fails, for any reason, to reach his decision in accordance with paragraph (1)

(a) any of the parties to the dispute may serve a fresh notice under paragraph 1 and shall request an adjudicator to act in accordance with paragraphs 2 to 7; and

(b) if requested by the new adjudicator and insofar as it is reasonably practicable, the parties shall supply him with copies of all documents which they had made available to the previous adjudicator.

(3) As soon as possible after he has reached a decision, the adjudicator shall deliver a copy of that decision to each of the parties to the contract.

Adjudicator's decision

20. The adjudicator shall decide the matters in dispute. He may take into account any other matters which the parties to the dispute agree should be within the scope of the adjudication or which are matters under the contract which he considers are necessarily connected with the dispute. In particular, he may–

(a) open up, revise and review any decision taken or any certificate given by any person referred to in the contract unless the contract states that the decision or certificate is final and conclusive,

(b) decide that any of the parties to the dispute is liable to make a payment under the contract (whether in sterling or some other currency) and, subject to section 111(4) of the Act, when that payment is due and the final date for payment,

(c) having regard to any term of the contract relating to the payment of interest decide the circumstances in which, and the rates at which, and the periods for which simple or compound rates of interest shall be paid.

21. In the absence of any directions by the adjudicator relating to the time for performance of his decision, the parties shall be required to comply with any decision of the adjudicator immediately on delivery of the decision to the parties in accordance with this paragraph.

22. If requested by one of the parties to the dispute, the adjudicator shall provide reasons for his decision.

Effects of the decision

23. – (1) In his decision, the adjudicator may, if he thinks fit, order any of the parties to comply peremptorily with his decision or any part of it.

(2) The decision of the adjudicator shall be binding on the parties, and they shall comply with it until the dispute is finally determined by legal proceedings, by arbitration (if the contract provides for arbitration or the parties otherwise agree to arbitration) or by agreement between the parties.

24. Section 42 of the Arbitration Act 1996 shall apply to this Scheme subject to the following modifications–

(a) in subsection (2) for the word 'tribunal' wherever it appears there shall be substituted the word 'adjudicator',
(b) in subparagraph (b) of subsection (2) for the words 'arbitral proceedings' there shall be substituted the word 'adjudication',
(c) subparagraph (c) of subsection (2) shall be deleted, and
(d) subsection (3) shall be deleted.

25. The adjudicator shall be entitled to the payment of such reasonable amount as he may determine by way of fees and expenses reasonably incurred by him. The parties shall be jointly and severally liable for any sum which remains outstanding following the making of any determination on how the payment shall be apportioned.

26. The adjudicator shall not be liable for anything done or omitted in the discharge or purported discharge of his functions as adjudicator unless the act or omission is in bad faith, and any employee or agent of the adjudicator shall be similarly protected from liability.

Crown copyright material is reproduced with the permission of the Controller of HMSO and the Queen's Printer for Scotland.

Appendix 3
Scheme for Construction Contracts (Scotland) Regulations 1998

SI 1998 No 687 (S.34)

CONSTRUCTION CONTRACTS

The Scheme for Construction Contracts (Scotland) Regulations 1998

Made	*6th March 1998*
Coming into force	*1st May 1998*

The Lord Advocate, in exercise of the powers conferred on him by sections 108(6), 114 and 146 of the Housing Grants, Construction and Regeneration Act 1996 and of all other powers enabling him in that behalf, having consulted such persons as he thinks fit, hereby makes the following Regulations, a draft of which has been laid before and has been approved by resolution of each House of Parliament:

Citation, commencement and extent

1. – (1) These Regulations may be cited as the Scheme for Construction Contracts (Scotland) Regulations 1998 and shall come into force at the end of the period of 8 weeks beginning with the day on which they are made.

(2) These Regulations extend to Scotland only.

Interpretation

2. In these Regulations, 'the Act' means the Housing Grants, Construction and Regeneration Act 1996.

The Scheme for Construction Contracts (Scotland)

3. Where a construction contract does not comply with the requirements of subsections (1) to (4) of section 108 of the Act, the adjudication provisions in Part I of the Schedule to these Regulations shall apply.

4. Where–
(a) the parties to a construction contract are unable to reach agreement for the purposes mentioned respectively in sections 109, 111 and 113 of the Act; or
(b) a construction contract does not make provision as required by section 110 of the Act,
the relevant provisions in Part II of the Schedule to these Regulations shall apply.

5. The provisions in the Schedule to these Regulations shall be the Scheme for Construction Contracts (Scotland) for the purposes of section 114 of the Act.

Hardie

Lord Advocate
Edinburgh

6th March 1998

SCHEDULE

Regulations 3 to 5

THE SCHEME FOR CONSTRUCTION CONTRACTS (SCOTLAND)

PART I – ADJUDICATION

Notice of intention to seek adjudication

1. – (1) Any party to a construction contract ('the referring party') may give written notice ('the notice of adjudication') of his intention to refer any dispute arising under the contract to adjudication.

(2) The notice of adjudication shall be given to every other party to the contract.

(3) The notice of adjudication shall set out briefly–

(a) the nature and a brief description of the dispute and of the parties involved;
(b) details of where and when the dispute has arisen;
(c) the nature of the redress which is sought; and
(d) the names and addresses of the parties to the contract (including, where appropriate, the addresses which the parties have specified for the giving of notices).

2. – (1) Following the giving of a notice of adjudication and subject to any agreement between the parties to the dispute as to who shall act as adjudicator–

(a) the referring party shall request the person (if any) specified in the contract to act as adjudicator;
(b) if no person is named in the contract or the person named has already indicated that he is unwilling or unable to act, and the contract provides for a specified nominating body to select a person, the referring party shall request the nominating body named in the contract to select a person to act as adjudicator; or
(c) where neither head (a) nor (b) above applies, or where the person referred to in (a) has already indicated that he is unwilling or unable to act and (b) does not apply, the

referring party shall request an adjudicator nominating body to select a person to act as adjudicator.

(2) A person requested to act as adjudicator in accordance with the provisions of sub-paragraph (1) shall indicate whether or not he is willing to act within two days of receiving the request.

(3) In this paragraph, and in paragraphs 5 and 6 below, 'an adjudicator nominating body' shall mean a body (not being a natural person and not being a party to the dispute) which holds itself out publicly as a body which will select an adjudicator when requested to do so by a referring party.

3. The request referred to in paragraphs 2, 5 and 6 shall be accompanied by a copy of the notice of adjudication.

4. Any person requested or selected to act as adjudicator in accordance with paragraphs 2, 5 or 6 shall be a natural person acting in his personal capacity. A person requested or selected to act as an adjudicator shall not be an employee of any of the parties to the dispute and shall declare any interest, financial or otherwise, in any matter relating to the dispute.

5. – (1) The nominating body referred to in paragraphs 2(1)(b) and 6(1)(b) or the adjudicator nominating body referred to in paragraphs 2(1)(c), 5(2)(b) and 6(1)(c) must communicate the selection of an adjudicator to the referring party within five days of receiving a request to do so.

(2) Where the nominating body or the adjudicator nominating body fails to comply with sub-paragraph (1), the referring party may–

(a) agree with the other party to the dispute to request a specified person to act as adjudicator; or
(b) request any other adjudicator nominating body to select a person to act as adjudicator.

(3) The person requested to act as adjudicator in accordance with the provisions of sub-paragraph (1) or (2) shall indicate whether or not he is willing to act within two days of receiving the request.

6. – (1) Where an adjudicator who is named in the contract indicates to the parties that he is unable or unwilling to act, or where he fails to respond in accordance with paragraph 2(2), the referring party may–

(a) request another person (if any) specified in the contract to act as adjudicator;
(b) request the nominating body (if any) referred to in the contract to select a person to act as adjudicator; or
(c) request any other adjudicator nominating body to select a person to act as adjudicator.

(2) The person requested to act in accordance with the provisions of sub-paragraph (1) shall indicate whether or not he is willing to act within two days of receiving the request.

7. – (1) Where an adjudicator has been selected in accordance with paragraphs 2, 5 or 6, the referring party shall, not later than seven days from the date of the notice of adjudication, refer the dispute in writing ('the referral notice') to the adjudicator.

(2) A referral notice shall be accompanied by copies of, or relevant extracts from, the construction contract and such other documents as the referring party intends to rely upon.

(3) The referring party shall, at the same time as he sends to the adjudicator the documents referred to in sub-paragraphs (1) and (2), send copies of those documents to every other party to the dispute.

8. – (1) The adjudicator may, with the consent of all the parties to those disputes, adjudicate at the same time on more than one dispute under the same contract.

(2) The adjudicator may, with the consent of all the parties to those disputes, adjudicate at the same time on related disputes under different contracts, whether or not one or more of those parties is a party to those disputes.

(3) All the parties in sub-paragraphs (1) and (2) respectively may agree to extend the period within which the adjudicator may reach a decision in relation to all or any of these disputes.

(4) Where an adjudicator ceases to act because a dispute is to be adjudicated on by another person in terms of this paragraph, that adjudicator's fees and expenses shall be determined and payable in accordance with paragraph 25.

9. – (1) An adjudicator may resign at any time on giving notice in writing to the parties to the dispute.

(2) An adjudicator must resign where the dispute is the same or substantially the same as one which has previously been referred to adjudication, and a decision has been taken in that adjudication.

(3) Where an adjudicator ceases to act under sub-paragraph (1)–

(a) the referring party may serve a fresh notice under paragraph 1 and shall request an adjudicator to act in accordance with paragraphs 2 to 7; and
(b) if requested by the new adjudicator and insofar as it is reasonably practicable, the parties shall supply him with copies of all documents which they had made available to the previous adjudicator.

(4) Where an adjudicator resigns in the circumstances mentioned in sub-paragraph (2), or where a dispute varies significantly from the dispute referred to him and for that reason he is not competent to decide it, that adjudicator's fees and expenses shall be determined and payable in accordance with paragraph 25.

10. Where any party to the dispute objects to the appointment of a particular person as adjudicator, that objection shall not invalidate the adjudicator's appointment nor any decision he may reach in accordance with paragraph 20.

11. – (1) The parties to a dispute may at any time agree to revoke the appointment of the adjudicator and in such circumstances the fees and expenses of that adjudicator shall, subject to sub-paragraph (2), be determined and payable in accordance with paragraph 25.

(2) Where the revocation of the appointment of the adjudicator is due to the default or misconduct of the adjudicator, the parties shall not be liable to pay the adjudicator's fees and expenses.

Powers of the adjudicator

12. The adjudicator shall–

(a) act impartially in carrying out his duties and shall do so in accordance with any relevant terms of the contract and shall reach his decision in accordance with the applicable law in relation to the contract; and

(b) avoid incurring unnecessary expense.

13. The adjudicator may take the initiative in ascertaining the facts and the law necessary to determine the dispute, and shall decide on the procedure to be followed in the adjudication. In particular, he may–

(a) request any party to the contract to supply him with such documents as he may reasonably require including, if he so directs, any written statement from any party to the contract supporting or supplementing the referral notice and any other documents given under paragraph 7(2);

(b) decide the language or languages to be used in the adjudication and whether a translation of any document is to be provided and, if so, by whom;

(c) meet and question any of the parties to the contract and their representatives;

(d) subject to obtaining any necessary consent from a third party or parties, make such site visits and inspections as he considers appropriate, whether accompanied by the parties or not;

(e) subject to obtaining any necessary consent from a third party or parties, carry out any tests or experiments;

(f) obtain and consider such representations and submissions as he requires, and, provided he has notified the parties of his intention, appoint experts, assessors or legal advisers;

(g) give directions as to the timetable for the adjudication, any deadlines, or limits as to the length of written documents or oral representations to be complied with; and

(h) issue other directions relating to the conduct of the adjudication.

14. The parties shall comply with any request or direction of the adjudicator in relation to the adjudication.

15. If, without showing sufficient cause, a party fails to comply with any request, direction or timetable of the adjudicator made in accordance with his powers, fails to produce any document or written statement requested by the adjudicator, or in any other way fails to comply with a requirement under these provisions relating to the adjudication, the adjudicator may–

(a) continue the adjudication in the absence of that party or of the document or written statement requested;
(b) draw such inferences from that failure to comply as may, in the adjudicator's opinion, be justified in the circumstances; and
(c) make a decision on the basis of the information before him, attaching such weight as he thinks fit to any evidence submitted to him outside any period he may have requested or directed.

16. – (1) Subject to any agreement between the parties to the contrary and to the terms of sub-paragraph (2), any party to the dispute may be assisted by, or represented by, such advisers or representatives (whether legally qualified or not) as he considers appropriate.

(2) Where the adjudicator is considering oral evidence or representations, a party to the dispute may not be represented by more than one person, unless the adjudicator gives directions to the contrary.

17. The adjudicator shall consider any relevant information submitted to him by any of the parties to the dispute and shall make available to them any information to be taken into account in reaching his decision.

18. The adjudicator and any party to the dispute shall not disclose to any other person any information or document provided to him in connection with the adjudication which the party supplying it has indicated is to be treated as confidential, except to the extent that it is necessary for the purposes of, or in connection with, the adjudication.

19. – (1) The adjudicator shall reach his decision not later than–

   (a) twenty eight days after the date of the referral notice mentioned in paragraph 7(1);

   (b) forty two days after the date of the referral notice if the referring party so consents; or

   (c) such period exceeding twenty eight days after the referral notice as the parties to the dispute may, after the giving of that notice, agree.

(2) Where the adjudicator fails, for any reason, to reach his decision in accordance with sub-paragraph (1)–

   (a) any of the parties to the dispute may serve a fresh notice under paragraph 1 and shall request an adjudicator to act in accordance with paragraphs 2 to 7; and

   (b) if requested by the new adjudicator and insofar as it is reasonably practicable, the parties shall supply him with copies of all documents which they had made available to the previous adjudicator.

(3) As soon as possible after he has reached a decision, the adjudicator shall deliver a copy of that decision to each of the parties to the contract.

Adjudicator's decision

20. – (1) The adjudicator shall decide the matters in dispute and may make a decision on different aspects of the dispute at different times.

(2) The adjudicator may take into account any other matters which the parties to the dispute agree should be within the scope of the adjudication or which are matters under the contract which he considers are necessarily connected with the dispute and, in particular, he may–

   (a) open up, review and revise any decision taken or any certificate given by any person referred to in the contract, unless the contract states that the decision or certificate is final and conclusive;

   (b) decide that any of the parties to the dispute is liable to make a payment under the contract (whether in sterling or some other currency) and, subject to section 111(4) of the Act, when that payment is due and the final date for payment;

(c) having regard to any term of the contract relating to the payment of interest, decide the circumstances in which, the rates at which, and the periods for which simple or compound rates of interest shall be paid.

21. In the absence of any directions by the adjudicator relating to the time for performance of his decision, the parties shall be required to comply with any decision of the adjudicator immediately on delivery of the decision to the parties in accordance with paragraph 19(3).

22. If requested by one of the parties to the dispute, the adjudicator shall provide reasons for his decision.

Effects of the decision

23. – (1) In his decision, the adjudicator may, if he thinks fit, order any of the parties to comply peremptorily with his decision or any part of it.

(2) The decision of the adjudicator shall be binding on the parties, and they shall comply with it, until the dispute is finally determined by legal proceedings, by arbitration (if the contract provides for arbitration or the parties otherwise agree to arbitration) or by agreement between the parties.

24. Where a party or the adjudicator wishes to register the decision for execution in the Books of Council and Session, any other party shall, on being requested to do so, forthwith consent to such registration by subscribing the decision before a witness.

25. – (1) The adjudicator shall be entitled to the payment of such reasonable amount as he may determine by way of fees and expenses incurred by him and the parties shall be jointly and severally liable to pay that amount to the adjudicator.

(2) Without prejudice to the right of the adjudicator to effect recovery from any party in accordance with sub-paragraph (1), the adjudicator may by direction determine the apportionment between the parties of liability for his fees and expenses.

26. The adjudicator shall not be liable for anything done or omitted in the discharge or purported discharge of his functions as adjudicator unless the act or omission is in bad faith, and any employee or agent of the adjudicator shall be similarly protected from liability.

Crown copyright material is reproduced with the permission of the Controller of HMSO and the Queen's Printer for Scotland.

Appendix 4
Scheme for Construction Contracts in Northern Ireland Regulations (Northern Ireland) 1999

STATUTORY RULES OF NORTHERN IRELAND

1999 No 32

CONSTRUCTION

The Scheme for Construction Contracts in Northern
Ireland Regulations (Northern Ireland) 1999

*To be laid before Parliament under paragraph 3(3) of Schedule 1
to the Northern Ireland Act 1974*

Made   *27th January 1999*

Coming into operation   1st June 1999

The Department of the Environment, in exercise of the
powers conferred on it by Articles 7(6), 13 and 16(1) of the
Construction Contracts (Northern Ireland) Order 1997, and
of every other power enabling it in that behalf, having
consulted with such persons as it thinks fit, thereby makes
the following Regulations:

Citation, commencement and interpretation

1. – (1) These Regulations may be cited as the Scheme for
Construction Contracts in Northern Ireland Regulations

(Northern Ireland) 1999 and shall come into operation on 1st June 1999.

(2) In these Regulations 'the 1997 Order' means the Construction Contracts (Northern Ireland) Order 1997.

The Scheme for Construction Contracts in Northern Ireland

2. Where a construction contract does not comply with the requirements of Article 7(1) to (4) of the 1997 Order, Part I of the Schedule shall apply.

3. Where–

(a) the parties to a construction contract are unable to reach agreement for the purposes mentioned respectively in Articles 8, 10 and 12 of the 1997 Order; or
(b) a construction contract does not make provision as required by Article 9 of the 1997 Order,

the relevant provisions in Part II of the Schedule shall apply.

4. The provisions in the Schedule shall be the Scheme.

Sealed with the Official Seal of the Department of the Environment on

L.S.
Trevor Pearson
Assistant Secretary

27th January 1999.

SCHEDULE

Regulations 2, 3 and 4

THE SCHEME

PART I – ADJUDICATION

Notice of Intention to seek Adjudication

1. – (1) Any party to a construction contract (the 'referring party') may give written notice (the 'notice of adjudication') of his intention to refer any dispute arising under the contract, to adjudication.

(2) The notice of adjudication shall be given to every other party to the contract.

(3) The notice of adjudication shall set out briefly –

(a) the nature and a brief description of the dispute and of the parties involved;
(b) details of where and when the dispute has arisen;
(c) the nature of the redress which is sought; and
(d) the names and addresses of the parties to the contract (including, where appropriate, the addresses which the parties have specified for the giving of notices).

2. – (1) Following the giving of a notice of adjudication and subject to any agreement between the parties to the dispute as to who shall act as adjudicator–

(a) the referring party shall request the person (if any) specified in the contract to act as adjudicator;
(b) if no person is named in the contract or the person named has already indicated that he is unwilling or unable to act, and the contract provides for a specified nominating body to select a person, the referring party shall request that nominating body named in the contract to select a person, the referring party shall request the nominating body named in the contract to select a person to act as adjudicator; or
(c) where neither paragraph (a) nor (b) applies, or where the person referred to in paragraph (a) has already indicated

that he is unwilling or unable to act and paragraph (*b*) does not apply, the referring party shall request an adjudicator nominating body to select a person to act as adjudicator.

(2) A person requested to act as adjudicator in accordance with sub-paragraph (1) shall indicate whether or not he is willing to act within 2 days of receiving the request.

(3) In this paragraph, and in paragraphs 5 and 6, an 'adjudicator nominating body' shall mean a body (not being an individual and not being a party to the dispute) which holds itself out publicly as a body which will select an adjudicator when requested to do so by a referring party.

3. The request referred to in paragraphs 2, 5 and 6 shall be accompanied by a copy of the notice of adjudication.

4. Any person requested or selected to act as adjudicator in accordance with paragraphs 2, 5 or 6 shall be an individual acting in his personal capacity. A person requested or selected to act as an adjudicator shall not be an employee of any of the parties to the dispute and shall declare any interest, financial or otherwise, in any matter relating to the dispute.

5. – (1) The nominating body referred to in paragraphs 2(1)(*b*) and 6(1)(*b*) or the adjudicator nominating body referred to in paragraphs 2(1)(*c*), 5(2)(*b*) and 6(1)(*c*) must communicate the selection of an adjudicator to the referring party within 5 days of receiving a request to do so.

(2) Where the nominating body or the adjudicator nominating body fails to comply with sub-paragraph (1), the referring party may–

(*a*) agree with the other party to the dispute to request a specified person to act as adjudicator; or
(*b*) request any other adjudicator nominating body to select a person to act as adjudicator.

(3) The person requested to act as adjudicator in accordance with sub-paragraphs (1) or (2) shall indicate whether or

not he is willing to act within 2 days of receiving the request.

6. – (1) Where an adjudicator who is named in the contract indicates to the parties that he is unable or unwilling to act, or where he fails to respond in accordance with paragraph 2(2), the referring party may–

(*a*) request another person (if any) specified in the contract to act as adjudicator;

(*b*) request the nominating body (if any) referred to in the contract to select a person to act as adjudicator; or

(*c*) request any other adjudicator nominating body to select a person to act as adjudicator.

(2) The person requested to act in accordance with sub-paragraph (1) shall indicate whether or not he is willing to act within 2 days of receiving the request.

7. – (1) Where an adjudicator has been selected in accordance with paragraphs 2, 5 or 6, the referring party shall, not later than 7 days from the date of the notice of adjudication, refer the dispute in writing (the 'referral notice') to the adjudicator.

(2) A referral notice shall be accompanied by copies of, or relevant extracts from, the construction contract and such other documents as the referring party intends to rely upon.

(3) The referring party shall, at the same time as he sends to the adjudicator the documents referred to in sub-paragraphs (1) and (2), send copies of those documents to every other party to the dispute.

8. – (1) The adjudicator may, with the consent of all the parties to those disputes, adjudicate at the same time on more than one dispute under the same contract.

(2) The adjudicator may, with the consent of all the parties to those disputes, adjudicate at the same time on related disputes under different contracts, whether or not one or more of those parties is a party to those disputes.

(3) All the parties in sub-paragraphs (1) and (2) respectively may agree to extend the period within which the adjudicator

may reach a decision in relation to all or any of these disputes.

(4) Where an adjudicator ceases to act because a dispute is to be adjudicated on by another person in terms of this paragraph, that adjudicator's fees and expenses shall be determined in accordance with paragraph 25.

9. – (1) An adjudicator may resign at any time on giving notice in writing to the parties to the dispute.

(2) An adjudicator must resign where the dispute is the same or substantially the same as one which has previously been referred to adjudication, and a decision has been taken in that adjudication.

(3) Where an adjudicator ceases to act under sub-paragraph (1)–

(a) the referring party may serve a fresh notice under paragraph 1 and shall request an adjudicator to act in accordance with paragraphs 2 to 7; and

(b) if requested by the new adjudicator and insofar as it is reasonably practicable, the parties shall supply him with copies of all documents which they had made available to the previous adjudicator.

(4) Where an adjudicator resigns in the circumstances referred to in sub-paragraph (2), or where a dispute varies significantly from the dispute referred to him in the referral notice and for that reason he is not competent to decide it, the adjudicator shall be entitled to the payment of such reasonable amount as he may determine by way of fees and expenses reasonably incurred by him. The parties shall be jointly and severally liable for any sum which remains outstanding following the making of any determination on how the payment shall be apportioned.

10. Where any party to the dispute objects to the appointment of a particular person as adjudicator, that objection shall not invalidate the adjudicator's appointment nor any decision he may reach in accordance with paragraph 20.

11. – (1) The parties to a dispute may at any time agree to revoke the appointment of the adjudicator. The adjudicator shall be entitled to the payment of such reasonable amount as he may determine by way of fees and expenses incurred by him. The parties shall be jointly and severally liable for any sum which remains outstanding following the making of any determination on how the payment shall be apportioned.

(2) Where the revocation of the appointment of the adjudicator is due to the default or misconduct of the adjudicator, the parties shall not be liable to apply the adjudicator's fees and expenses.

Powers of the adjudicator

12. The adjudicator shall–

(a) act impartially in carrying out his duties and shall do so in accordance with any relevant terms of the contract and shall reach his decision in accordance with the applicable law in relation to the contract; and

(b) avoid incurring unnecessary expense.

13. The adjudicator may take the initiative in ascertaining the facts and the law necessary to determine the dispute, and shall decide on the procedure to be followed in the adjudication. In particular he may–

(a) request any part [sic] to the contract to supply him with such documents as he may reasonably require including, if he so directs, any written statement from any party to the contract supporting or supplementing the referral notice and any other documents given under paragraph 7(2);

(b) decide the language or languages to be used in the adjudication and whether a translation of any document is to be provided and if so by whom;

(c) meet and question any of the parties to the contract and their representatives;

(d) subject to obtaining any necessary consent from a third party, make such site visits and inspections as he considers appropriate, whether accompanied by the parties or not;

(e) subject to obtaining any necessary consent from a third party, carry out any tests or experiments;

(f) obtain and consider such representations and submissions as he requires, and, provided he has notified the parties of his intention, appoint experts, assessors or legal advisers;

(g) give directions as to the timetable for the adjudication, any deadlines, or limits as to the length of written document or oral representations to be complied with; and

(h) issue other directions relating to the conduct of the adjudication.

14. The parties shall comply with any request or direction of the adjudicator in relation to the adjudication.

15. If, without showing sufficient cause, a party fails to comply with any request, direction or timetable of the adjudicator made in accordance with his powers, fails to produce any document or written statement requested by the adjudicator, or in any other way fails to comply with a requirement under these provisions relating to the adjudication, the adjudicator may–

(a) continue the adjudication in the absence of that party or of the document or written statement requested,

(b) draw such inferences from that failure to comply as circumstances may, in the adjudicator's opinion, be justified; and

(c) make a decision on the basis of the information before him attaching such weight as he thinks fit to any evidence submitted to him outside any period he may have requested or directed.

16. – (1) Subject to any agreement between the parties to the contrary, and to the terms of sub-paragraph (2), any party to the dispute may be assisted by, or represented by, such advisers or representatives (whether legally qualified or not) as he considers appropriate.

(2) Where the adjudicator is considering oral evidence or representations, a party to the dispute may not be represented by more than one person, unless the adjudicator gives directions to the contrary.

17. The adjudicator shall consider any relevant information submitted to him by any of the parties to the dispute and shall make available to them any information to be taken into account in reaching his decision.

18. The adjudicator and any party to the dispute shall not disclose to any other person any information or document provided to him in connection with the adjudication which the party supplying it has indicated is to be treated as confidential, except to the extent that it is necessary for the purposes of, or in connection with, the adjudication.

19. – (1) The adjudicator shall reach his decision not later than–

(*a*) 28 days after the date of the referral notice mentioned in paragraph 7(1);
(*b*) 42 days after the date of the referral notice if the referring party so consents; or
(*c*) such period exceeding 28 days after the referral notice as the parties to the dispute may, after the giving of that notice, agree.

(2) Where the adjudicator fails, for any reason, to reach his decision in accordance with sub-paragraph (1)–

(*a*) any of the parties to the dispute may serve a fresh notice under paragraph 1 and shall request an adjudicator to act in accordance with paragraphs 2 to 7; and
(*b*) if requested by the new adjudicator and insofar as it is reasonably practicable, the parties shall supply him with copies of all documents which they had made available to the previous adjudicator.

(3) As soon as possible after he has reached a decision, the adjudicator shall deliver a copy of that decision to each of the parties to the contract.

Adjudicator's decision

20. The adjudicator shall decide the matters in dispute. He may take into account any other matters which the parties to the dispute agree should be within the scope of the adjudication or which are matters under the contract which he considers are necessarily connected with the dispute. In particular, he may–

(a) open up, revise and review any decision taken or any certificate given by any person referred to in the contract unless the contract states that the decision or certificate is final and conclusive;

(b) decide that any of the parties to the dispute is liable take a payment under the contract (whether in sterling or some other currency) and, subject to Article 10(4) of the 1997 Order, when that payment is due and the final date for payment;

(c) having regard to any term of the contract relating to the payment of interest decide the circumstances in which, and the rates at which, and the periods for which simple or compound rates of interest shall be paid.

21. In the absence of any directions by the adjudicator relating to the time for performance of his decision, the parties shall be required to comply with any decision of the adjudicator immediately on delivery of the decision to the parties in accordance with this paragraph.

22. If requested by one of the parties to the dispute, the adjudicator shall provide reasons for his decision.

Effects of the decision

23. – (1) In his decision, the adjudicator may, if he thinks fit, order any of the parties to comply peremptorily with his decision or any part of it.

(2) The decision of the adjudicator shall be binding on the parties, and they shall comply with it until the dispute is finally determined by legal proceedings, by arbitration (if the contract provides for arbitration or the parties otherwise agree to arbitration) or by agreement between the parties.

24. Section 42 of the Arbitration Act 1996 shall apply to this Scheme subject to the following modifications–

(a) for the word 'tribunal' wherever it appears there shall be substituted the word 'adjudicator';

(b)   in paragraph (b) of sub-section (2) for the words 'arbitral proceedings' there shall be substituted the word 'adjudication';

(c)   paragraph (c) of sub-section (2) shall be deleted; and

(d)   sub-section (3) shall be deleted.

25. The adjudicator shall be entitled to the payment of such reasonable amount as he may determine by way of fees and expenses reasonably incurred by him. The parties shall be jointly and severally liable for any sum which remains outstanding following the making of any determination on how the payment shall be apportioned.

26. The adjudicator shall not be liable for anything done or omitted in the discharge or purported discharge of his functions as adjudicator unless the act or omission is in bad faith, and any employee or agent of the adjudicator shall be similarly protected from liability.

Crown copyright material is reproduced with the permission of the Controller of HMSO and the Queen's Printer for Scotland.

Appendix 5
Construction Contracts (England and Wales) Exclusion Order 1998

SI 1998 No 648

CONSTRUCTION, ENGLAND AND WALES

The Construction Contracts (England and Wales) Exclusion Order 1998

Made   *6th March 1998*

Coming into force in
accordance with article 1(1)

The Secretary of State, in exercise of the powers conferred on him by sections 106(1)(b) and 146(1) of the Housing Grants, Construction and Regeneration Act 1996 and of all other powers enabling him in that behalf, hereby makes the following Order, a draft of which has been laid before and approved by resolution of, each House of Parliament:

Citation, commencement and extent

1. – (1) This Order may be cited as the Construction Contracts (England and Wales) Exclusion Order 1998 and shall come into force at the end of the period of 8 weeks beginning with the day on which it is made ('the commencement date').

(2) This Order shall extend to England and Wales only.

Interpretation

2. In this Order, 'Part II' means Part II of the Housing Grants, Construction and Regeneration Act 1996.

Agreements under statute

3. A construction contract is excluded from the operation of Part II if it is –

(a) an agreement under section 38 (power of highway authorities to adopt by agreement) or section 278 (agreements as to execution of works) of the Highways Act 1980;

(b) an agreement under section 106 (planning obligations), 106A (modification or discharge of planning obligations) or 299A (Crown planning obligations) of the Town and Country Planning Act 1990;

(c) an agreement under section 104 of the Water Industry Act 1991 (agreements to adopt sewer, drain or sewage disposal works); or

(d) an externally financed development agreement within the meaning of section 1 of the National Health Service (Private Finance) Act 1997 (powers of NHS Trusts to enter into agreements).

Private finance initiative

4. – (1) A construction contract is excluded from the operation of Part II if it is a contract entered into under the private finance initiative, within the meaning given below.

(2) A contract is entered into under the private finance initiative if all the following conditions are fulfilled –

(a) it contains a statement that it is entered into under that initiative or, as the case may be, under a project applying similar principles;

(b) the consideration due under the contract is determined at least in part by reference to one or more of the following –

(i) the standards attained in the performance of a service, the provision of which is the principal purpose or one of the principal purposes for which the building or structure is constructed;

(ii) the extent, rate or intensity of use of all or any part of the building or structure in question; or

(iii) the right to operate any facility in connection with the building or structure in question; and

(c) one of the parties to the contract is–

    (i)   a Minister of the Crown;

    (ii)   a department in respect of which appropriation accounts are required to be prepared under the Exchequer and Audit Departments Act 1866;

    (iii) any other authority or body whose accounts are required to be examined and certified by or are open to the inspection of the Comptroller and Auditor General by virtue of an agreement entered into before the commencement date or by virtue of any enactment;

    (iv) any authority or body listed in Schedule 4 to the National Audit Act 1983 (nationalised industries and other public authorities);

    (v)   a body whose accounts are subject to audit by auditors appointed by the Audit Commission;

    (vi) the governing body or trustees of a voluntary school within the meaning of section 31 of the Education Act 1996 (county schools and voluntary schools), or

    (vii) a company wholly owned by any of the bodies described in paragraphs (i) to (v).

Finance agreements

5. – (1) A construction contract is excluded from the operation of Part II if it is a finance agreement, within the meaning given below.

(2) A contract is a finance agreement if it is any one of the following –

(a) any contract of insurance;

(b) any contract under which the principal obligations include the formation or dissolution of a company, unincorporated association or partnership;

(c) any contract under which the principal obligations include the creation or transfer of securities or any right or interest in securities;

(d) any contract under which the principal obligations include the lending of money;

(e) any contract under which the principal obligations include an undertaking by a person to be responsible as surety for the debt or default of another person, including a fidelity bond, advance payment bond, retention bond or performance bond.

Development agreements

6. – (1) A construction contract is excluded from the operation of Part II if it is a development agreement, within the meaning given below.

(2) A contract is a development agreement if it includes provision for the grant or disposal of a relevant interest in the land on which take place the principal construction operations to which the contract relates.

(3) In paragraph (2) above, a relevant interest in land means –

(a) a freehold; or

(b) a leasehold for a period which is to expire no earlier than 12 months after the completion of the construction operations under the contract.

Signed by authority of the Secretary of State

Nick Raynsford

Parliamentary Under-Secretary of State, Department of the Environment, Transport and the Regions

6th March 1998

Appendix 6
Construction Contracts (Scotland) Exclusion Order 1998

SI 1998 No 686 (S.33)

CONSTRUCTION CONTRACTS

The Construction Contracts (Scotland) Exclusion Order 1998

Made	*6th March 1998*
Coming into force	*1st May 1998*

The Secretary of State, in exercise of the powers conferred on him by sections 106(1)(b) and 146(1) of the Housing Grants, Construction and Regeneration Act 1996 and of all other powers enabling him in that behalf, hereby makes the following Order, a draft of which has been laid before, and approved by resolution of, each House of Parliament:

Citation, commencement and extent

1. – (1) This Order may be cited as the Construction Contracts (Scotland) Exclusion Order 1998 and shall come into force at the end of the period of 8 weeks beginning with the day on which it is made.

(2) This Order shall extend to Scotland only.

Interpretation

2. In this Order, 'Part II' means Part II of the Housing Grants, Construction and Regeneration Act 1996.

Agreements under statute

3. A construction contract is excluded from the operation of Part II if it is–

(a) an agreement under section 48 (contributions towards expenditure on constructing or improving roads) of the Roads (Scotland) Act 1984;

(b) an agreement under section 75 (agreements regulating development or use of land) or 246 (agreements relating to Crown land) of the Town and Country Planning (Scotland) Act 1997;

(c) an agreement under section 8 (agreements as to provision of sewers etc. for new premises) of the Sewerage (Scotland) Act 1968; or

(d) an externally financed development agreement within the meaning of section 1 (powers of NHS Trusts to enter into agreements) of the National Health Service (Private Finance) Act 1997.

Private finance initiative

4. – (1) A construction contract is excluded from the operation of Part II if it is a contract entered into under the private finance initiative, within the meaning given below.

(2) A contract is entered into under the private finance initiative if all the following conditions are fulfilled:–

(a) it contains a statement that it is entered into under that initiative or, as the case may be, under a project applying similar principles;

(b) the consideration due under the contract is determined at least in part by reference to one or more of the following:–

(i) the standards attained in the performance of a service, the provision of which is the principal purpose or one of the principal purposes for which the building or structure is constructed;

(ii) the extent, rate or intensity of use of all or any part of the building or structure in question; or

(iii) the right to operate any facility in connection with the building or structure in question; and

(c) one of the parties to the contract is–
  (i) a Minister of the Crown;
  (ii) a department in respect of which appropriation accounts are required to be prepared under the Exchequer and Audit Departments Act 1866;
  (iii) any other authority or body whose accounts are required to be examined and certified by or are open to the inspection of the Comptroller and Auditor General by virtue of an agreement entered into before the date on which this Order comes into force, or by virtue of any enactment;
  (iv) any authority or body listed in Schedule 4 (nationalised industries and other public authorities) to the National Audit Act 1983;
  (v) a body whose accounts are subject to audit by auditors appointed by the Accounts Commission for Scotland;
  (vi) a water and sewerage authority established under section 62 (new water and sewerage authorities) of the Local Government etc. (Scotland) Act 1994;
  (vii) the board of management of a self-governing school within the meaning of section 1(3) (duty of Secretary of State to maintain self-governing schools) of the Self-Governing Schools etc. (Scotland) Act 1989; or
  (viii) a company wholly owned by any of the bodies described in heads (i) to (v) above.

Finance agreements

5. – (1) A construction contract is excluded from the operation of Part II if it is a finance agreement, within the meaning given below.

(2) A contract is a finance agreement if it is any one of the following:–
(a) any contract of insurance;
(b) any contract under which the principal obligations include the formation or dissolution of a company, unincorporated association or partnership;
(c) any contract under which the principal obligations include the creation or transfer of securities or any right or interest in securities;

(d) any contract under which the principal obligations include the lending of money;

(e) any contract under which the principal obligations include an undertaking by a person to be responsible as surety for the debt or default of another person, including a fidelity bond, advance payment bond, retention bond or performance bond.

Development agreements

6. – (1) A construction contract is excluded from the operation of Part II if it is a development agreement, within the meaning given below.

(2) A contract is a development agreement if it includes provision for the grant or disposal of a relevant interest in the land on which take place the principal construction operations to which the contract relates.

(3) In paragraph (2) above, a relevant interest in land means–

(a) ownership; or

(b) a tenant's interest under a lease for a period which is to expire no earlier than 12 months after the completion of the construction operations under the contract.

Calum MacDonald

Parliamentary Under Secretary of State, Scottish Office
St Andrew's House, Edinburgh

6th March 1998

Appendix 7
Construction Contracts Exclusion Order (Northern Ireland) 1999

STATUTORY RULES OF NORTHERN IRELAND

1999 No 33

CONSTRUCTION

The Construction Contracts Exclusion Order
(Northern Ireland) 1999

*To be laid before Parliament under paragraph 3(3) of Schedule 1
to the Northern Ireland Act 1974*

Made   *27th January 1999*

Coming into operation   *1st June 1999*

The Department of the Environment, in exercise of the powers conferred on it by Article 5(1)(*b*) of the Construction Contracts (Northern Ireland) Order 1997, and of every other power enabling it in that behalf, hereby makes the following Order:

Citation, commencement and interpretation

1. – (1) This Order may be cited as the Construction Contracts Exclusion Order (Northern Ireland) 1999 and shall come into operation on 1st June 1999.

(2) In this Order, 'the 1997 Order' means the Construction Contracts (Northern Ireland) Order 1997.

Agreements under statute

2. A construction contract is excluded from the operation of the 1997 Order if it is –

(*a*) an agreement under Article 3(4C) (works for the improvement of a public road joined by a private street) or Article 32 (agreement for carrying out street works in a private street) of the Private Streets (Northern Ireland) Order 1980;

(*b*) an agreement under Article 122 of the Roads (Northern Ireland) Order 1993 (execution of works by Department at expense of another);

(*c*) an agreement under Article 40 of the Planning (Northern Ireland) Order 1991 (agreements facilitating, regulating or restricting development or use of land);

(*d*) an externally financed development agreement under Article 3 of the Health and Personal Social Services (Private Finance) (Northern Ireland) Order 1997 (powers of Health and Social Services trusts to enter into agreements); or

(*e*) an agreement under Article 17(4) of the Water and Sewerage Services (Northern Ireland) Order 1973 (applications for water or sewerage services).

Private finance initiative

3. – (1) A construction contract is excluded from the operation of the 1997 Order if it is a contract entered into under the private finance initiative.

(2) For the purposes of paragraph (1), a contract is entered into under the private finance initiative if all the following conditions are fulfilled –

(*a*) it contains a statement that it is entered into under that initiative;

(*b*) the consideration due under the contract is determined at least in part by reference to one or more of the following –

(i) the standards attained in the performance of a service, the provision of which is the principal purpose or one of the principal purposes for which the building or structure is constructed;

(ii) the extent, rate or intensity of use of all or any part of the building or structure in question; or

(iii) the right to operate any facility in connection with the building or structure in question; and

(c) one of the parties to the contract is –

(i) a Minister of the Crown or the head of a Northern Ireland department;

(ii) a Northern Ireland department;

(iii) any other authority or body whose accounts are required to be examined and certified by or are open to the inspection of the Comptroller and Auditor General for Northern Ireland by virtue of an agreement entered into before the coming into operation of this Order or by virtue of any statutory provision;

(iv) the Northern Ireland Transport Holding Company;

(v) a body whose accounts are subject to audit by auditors appointed under section 74 of the Local Government Act (Northern Ireland) 1972, or Article 90 of the Health and Personal Social Services (Northern Ireland) Order 1972;

(vi) the managers or trustees of a voluntary school or the managers or trustees of a grant-maintained integrated school within the meaning of the Education and Libraries (Northern Ireland) Order 1986;

(vii) a company wholly owned by any of the bodies described in heads (i) to (v).

Finance agreements

4. – (1) A construction contract is excluded from the operation of the 1997 Order if it is a finance agreement.

(2) For the purposes of paragraph (1), a contract is a finance agreement if it is any one of the following –

(a) any contract of insurance;

(b) any contract under which the principal obligations include the formation or dissolution of a company, unincorporated association or partnership;

(c) any contract under which the principal obligations include the creation or transfer of securities or any right of interest in securities;

(d) any contract under which the principal obligations include the lending of money;
(e) any contract under which the principal obligations include an undertaking by a person to be responsible as surety for the debt or default of another person, including a fidelity bond, advance payment bond, retention bond or performance bond.

Development agreements

5. – (1) A construction contract is excluded from the operation of the 1997 Order if it is a development agreement.

(2) For the purposes of paragraph (1), a contract is a development agreement if it includes provision for the disposal of a relevant estate in the land on which take place the principal construction operations to which the contract relates.

(3) In paragraph (2) a relevant estate in land means –

(a) a freehold; or
(b) a leasehold for a period which is to expire no earlier than 12 months after the completion of the construction operations under the contract.

Sealed with the Official Seal of the Department of the Environment on

L.S.
Trevor Pearson
Assistant Secretary

27th January 1999.

Crown copyright material is reproduced with the permission of the Controller of HMSO and the Queen's Printer for Scotland.

Index

The Case in Point series

The *Case in Point* series is an exciting new set of concise practical guides to legal issues in land, property and construction. Written for the property professional, they get straight to the key issues in a refreshingly jargon-free style.

Areas covered:

Negligence in Valuation and Surveys
Stock code: 6388
Published: December 2002

Party Walls
Stock code: 7269
Published: May 2004

Service Charges
Stock code: 7272
Published: June 2004

Estate Agency
Stock code: 7472
Published: July 2004

Rent Review
Stock code: 8531
Published: May 2005

Expert Witness
Stock code: 8842
Published: August 2005

Lease Renewal
Stock code: 8711
Published: August 2005

Publishing soon:
VAT in Property and Construction
Stock code: 8840

If you would like to be kept informed when new *Case in Point* titles are published, please e-mail **rbmarketing@rics.org.uk**

How to order:

All RICS Books titles can be ordered direct by:

☎ Telephoning 0870 333 1600 (Option 3)
⌐ Online at www.ricsbooks.com
✉ E-mail mailorder@rics.org.uk